Horses and Courses

HORSES AND COURSES

A Pictorial History of Racing

David Hedges

Photographs by Fred Mayer

Foreword by John Hislop

A Studio Book

The Viking Press · New York

This book was prepared and
produced by Niklaus Flüeler,
was designed by Roland Gfeller-
Corthesy, and manufactured by
City-Druck AG, Glattbrugg,
Zurich.

Printed and bound
in Switzerland

Published in 1972
by The Viking Press, Inc.

625 Madison Avenue,
New York, N.Y. 10022

Published simultaneously in
Canada by
The Macmillan Company of
Canada Limited

SBN 670-37953-0

Library of Congress catalog card
number: 72-81671

Foreword

by John Hislop

While the shape of racing has changed markedly over the years, it has retained the essential qualities which have formed its great attraction.

It is a trial of racing merit, not only between one horse and another, but of speed, stamina, courage, soundness, constitution, temperament and all the many factors that combine to make the Thoroughbred at his best. It is also a trial of the representatives of the studs of different individuals, districts and nations. Indeed, the Turf is an interest which knows no boundaries.

Even in the far off days when travel was an ordeal at which the modern voyager, human or equine, would quail, horses were journeying from all parts of the world to race against each other.

A victory of the U.S.A. in The Derby is by no means a post-war phenomenon. As long ago as 1881 the race went across the Atlantic, when the winner was the American colt, Iroquois, owned by Mr. Lorillard and ridden by Fred Archer; while even earlier, in 1865, Count Lagrange's Gladiateur took the triple-crown, thereby earning himself the soubriquet of "The Avenger of Waterloo"; and thirteen years later, the brilliant Hungarian mare, Kincsem, who raced all over Europe and never met defeat, won the Goodwood Cup.

With the arrival of air travel the world, both on and off the Turf, has shrunk. Journeys which once represented weeks or months are now a matter of hours: it is as easy for a horse to go from Newmarket to Longchamp as it is for one to go from Chantilly to Epsom; and a journey to the U.S.A. from Europe offers no fears, as evinced in the victories of Wilwyn, Match III, Sir Ivor and others in the Washington D.C. International at Laurel Park, a race which went as far afield as Australia in 1958, when it was awarded to Sailor's Guide.

This has increased the international aspect of the Turf, not only as regards racing but also in respect of breeding. Mares travel from one continent to another to visit stallions, and pedigrees have become increasingly less distinctive of any one country. The champion of today invariably has an international pedigree.

This interchange of blood has had a beneficial effect on the Thoroughbred in general, since it has enabled the fullest use to be made of influences productive of different environments.

The wide scope of this book is therefore particularly appropriate to the age in which we live, and its value lies not only in the nature of the text and quality of presentation but also in the international field which it covers. Those who read it will be taken, as it were, on a world tour of racing, gaining an understanding of many different aspects of the sport and the literary pleasure of fresh fields and pastures new.

One of the most entertaining sides of racing is trying to assess the relative merit of horses of different eras and from different countries. Perforce, this is almost invariably a matter of personal opinion and considerable argument. In the chapter, Twelve of the Best, David Hedges names his leading dozen of the best horses in Turf history.

Readers will have the enjoyment of comparing this list with those of their own choice, but none can quibble at the inclusion of such as St. Simon, Ormonde and Ribot.

Other features deserving mention are the chapters on crime and on travelling horses.

The author is to be commended upon the widespread and painstaking work which has gone to produce this attractive and informative work.

Preliminaries, Tokyo

The finish, Auteuil, Paris

After the race, Palermo, Buenos Aires

To the winner—Baghdad Note's Melbourne Cup, 1970

The Racing Game

A man cannot call himself an expert on horse-racing today if he has studied only the sport within his own country. Racing has become international. The great blood-lines have spread out, crossed oceans and continents and often returned refreshed to the country of their origin.

This book is not intended to be a heavyweight manual for the expert, but aims to take you on a tour of the racecourses of the world and to examine some of the changes that have taken place in racing and breeding during the past twenty years, and which continue...

The author has jogged around the racing world a little, and enjoyed the sport in a variety of countries and surroundings. In the following pages the intention is to go racing again, to revive memories of horses and courses seen, and to talk, too, of those we wish we had seen. There will be pauses to take a closer look at beautiful racecourses, great horses, and to gossip about characters and crimes, in an attempt to evoke the colour and texture of racing in different lands.

Racing is now a travelling game. The champion horses themselves have felt beneath their hooves the grass of Royal Ascot and of Longchamp, the dirt of the American tracks. They travel thousands of miles by air and road to challenge the best from other countries.

Jockeys from Wagga Wagga and New York City and Lambourn, when they meet, can talk knowledgeably among themselves about the great and not so great horses of many countries, their breeding, their trainers and the race tracks on which they run.

"You know how there's two sorts of going now on the grass course at Laurel, it's different on the old turf in the straight ..."

"You remember how Hutchy was nearly put over the rail by that German jock the time we rode in Sweden. The name of the race! It was as long as the track ..."

"No, I never rode at Wanganui, but the trainer says it's like all those sharp little N.Z. country courses ..."

"You wait till you see the new jockeys' room–it's as good as the powder room in the London Hilton, though I've never ..."

The racecourses are remembered by the jockeys for success or failure, the banking of this turn, the near fall at that bend, the taste of the cup of coffee in the jockeys' room, the professional we-know-what's-going-on-look on the faces of the stewards.

When the riders are out there on the track racing, they are in a world of their own, the whip of the wind and their concentration on the job cut out the noise of the crowd, make them forget that thousands of people within a few hundred yards are variously and vitally interested in everything they do.

It is only when they pull up their horses and turn to jog back to unsaddle that the contact leaps back, like sound restored to a silent television set.

An empty racecourse looks neat and tidy and newly washed in the early morning sunshine, but it is in the afternoon, with people injected and horses and more people, that it comes to life.

Racecourses mean people–betting, shouting, chewing, spitting, drinking, forgetting, counting their money, cursing their wives. They come from every walk of life. Some may have begged or borrowed their entrance money and enough to have a bet. Some may have stolen it. Others could afford to buy up the race track. But wherever they come from, if you picked them up and put them down on another race track the other side of the world they would be at home. There would be different forms of betting, different tickets to handle, a different language perhaps, but they would recognise themselves in the crowd around them, and the people they are always meeting on their home race track. They would recognise the intense concentration, almost of prayer, that the racegoer wraps himself in as he peers at his newspaper and his race card and moves towards the parimutuel windows.

Racegoing is a bond. The veteran British owner Lord Rosebery once said, "It is the best way of starting a conversation that I know." In a bar or a boat or a railway train, there will always be someone ready to exchange opinions with you on horse racing, to compare the merits of horses of yesterday and today and to talk about the respective qualities of race tracks. Much of the conversation will hinge on what won yesterday and what will win tomorrow, but not all–for finding the winner is only a part, albeit vital, in the rich world that is centred on the race tracks.

Among the memories that come crowding back to us are not just of big names and big races, but of the little things as well–the bright blue umbrellas over the bookmakers' stands at Flemington, Australia; the top-hatted starter riding his handsome hack to the start in front of 50,000 people at Royal Ascot, England; the decrepit limousine used for the same job at Rotorua, New Zealand.

At Caracas, Venezuela, at the invitation of one of the television producers, we walked into a little room at the top of the brilliantly designed stand, to see the live broadcast of racing in progress.

Finish of V. R. C. Hotham Handicap
Flemington, November 3rd, 1956
'Pandie Sun' (on rails), 'Ark Royal' (centre), 'Fighting Force' (outside)
Result: TRIPLE DEAD HEAT
Official "Camera-Graph" for WIN

On the line—top photo shows one of the few triple dead heats recorded since the introduction of the photo finish camera. The judge's magnifying glass could not seperate Pandie Sun, Ark Royal and Fighting Force at the end of the V.R.C. Hotham Handicap, Flemington, Australia, 1965.

There, high in the stands above the pulsating crowd, they had all the stock needed for the commercials. Perched everywhere on ledges were bottles of scotch, packets of detergent, boxes of candy, packs of nylon stockings.

At that moment the stewards were dealing with a highly contentious objection, while the racing fans below kept up an almost continuous piercing whistle of protest. The din transformed to dead silence as the loudspeakers announced the stewards' decision, to shrill out once more, backed by vociferous booing, at an unpopular decision. The whole programme was delayed, so that by the time the last race was run, the sun had long since disappeared behind the high mountains that back the track. It was so dark that the only time the horses could be seen was when they flashed through the strip of light provided to illuminate the finishing line.

Epsom, England, on Derby Day presents a spectacle unencountered in other parts of the world, with tens of thousands of people teeming on the hill in the centre of the course, intermingled with temporary stands and bars, huge advertising hoardings, caravans, bookmakers, tic-tac men in white gloves, hot gospellers with banners—a carnival. Waves of music from the roundabouts and dodgems infiltrate across the track, bursting in on the proper affairs of the turf in the staid enclosure reserved for owners, trainers and jockeys.

And there are always dogs at Epsom which get into the picture, sometimes two or three of them putting up a hopeless chase of the horses, who are safely guarded from their canine pursuers by a wire fence. For a few hundred yards, as the horses come down the hill and round Tattenham Corner into the straight you can see, while trying to concentrate on the race through your binoculars, a scurry of white and brown as a little bevy of dogs flashes through the clear space behind the crowd at the rails, until finally they turn and wheel away to find some less energetic form of mischief than trying to keep pace with an Hyperion or a Sea Bird.

At Epsom, too, gentlemen in grey top hats and striped trousers stand with legs apart and spoon eels in aspic out of little bowls, spitting the bones on the ground with an accuracy necessary to preserve the neatness of their hired suits.

At Ascot of royal splendour, where many go to be seen rather than to watch racing (which is a pity, as the racing is superb) there is an old horse which clops up and down from the railway station to the course, hauling a landau filled with rather self-conscious racegoers on the way to the meeting; and flushed celebrants making a gesture on the way back.

During the racing, the eye is occasionally caught

"Here they come", Derby day, Epsom, 1878, by C. Green (top), "Race meeting at Newmarket" by Peter Tillemans, 1684–1734 (centre).

by children at play in the open-air playground, stopping and running to the rails to watch as the horses thunder towards the stands–racegoers of the future, momentarily discarding the rocking horse for the real thing of tomorrow.

Ascot has its fantastic hats, worn by ladies determined to make the evening papers and the glossies, and so too does Melbourne on Cup Day. A continuous stream of helicopters flies in race-goers, hopping over the traffic jams, landing them close to where the kilted pipe band is forming up for the pre-race parade. Wives segregated to the ladies' stand chat nineteen to the dozen, wondering which bar their husbands are patronising in the men-only section of the stands. The commentator, accurate but almost incomprehensible to the uninitiated, winds himself up into his quick-fire, bet-you-couldn't-do-better-than-this act. Racegoers walk around with their ears pressed to transistor radios as they listen to race descriptions from other meetings. The Australian likes a good horse. He also likes a good bet, and if there is not enough action in eight races at Melbourne, he can always pass a bet on the inter-track network to another meeting.

Although Americans are sometimes surprised at the pre-eminence that foreigners are liable to accord to Laurel Race Course, Maryland, so well known abroad because of its international race, it will always conjure up memories for us, of the colourful characters, both equine and human, assembled from many lands for the annual running of the Washington D.C. International Stakes.

The fullest flavour of the event is drawn from watching the early morning work, when owners, trainers, journalists and cameramen from all over the world hang around the gap in the rails on the back stretch, watching the final gallops of Derby winners from South America and Ireland, Russian horses ridden by grinning, well-fed jockeys, a group of gloomy Frenchmen, shrugging their shoulders at questions as to whether the going will suit their horse, a Japanese animal with golden mane and tail, stepping out with pointed toe like a circus horse.

When the horses have gone back to their stables, then comes breakfast of orange juice, eggs, sunny-side up, french-fried and coffee in the stable area kitchen, where English lords, Canadian millionaires and journalists sit down among the work riders, some still crash-helmeted, for a breakfast that always tastes the better for that appetiser of clean Maryland fall air.

Aqueduct, New York, is a vast modern race-track with stands covering seven acres, where its fans bet up to 5½ million dollars in one day. We recall, in the large, strip-lit money-counting room, the chatter of the counting machine as it totted up astronomic assemblies of dollar and higher denomination bills, and the super efficiency of the stewards, based on an experience of over 2,000 races in the year, upon whose decisions the destiny of vast sums of money depends. Aqueduct goes like clockwork, and provides relaxation for millions, but is perhaps a supermarket, a computer, a vast impersonal racing machine for the purpose of placing bets. For all its comfort, its efficiency, it seems to us to have lost, somewhere along the road to luxury, a part of the savour of horse-racing.

The charm has not gone out of the rebuilt Longchamp, where Parisians now watch their racing from six lavish modern stands, which were built to one side of the attractive but uncomfortable old buildings and then inched in on rails to take the place of the older stands. While families, from grandmother downwards, sit around under the trees at the back of the stands fanning themselves with those floppy race programmes the French favour, men with flimsy slips of paper bearing the latest betting odds on the parimutuel go through the crowds calling "Dernier, dernier" and handing them out to clients; the lively crowd shout words of encouragement as the jockeys ride out through a gap between the stands onto the course. And the jockeys smile occasionally, knowing that they will have to return through a hail of stinging invective, whistling and booing, if they appear to do anything wrong in the race.

There are memories too, of horses, possessing as many facets of character as the people who watch them in action on the track. Horses like America's Kelso, who won nearly two million dollars in eight seasons. We say America's and not Mrs. Richard du Pont's Kelso, because a horse of such a calibre belongs to everyone. He had the star quality to draw spontaneous applause from a race track crowd at the very mention of his name on the public address system, to attract his own fan mail, to prompt the production of Kelso lump sugar neatly wrapped in the stable colours of grey and yellow.

But not everyone was a Kelso fan, and indeed admiration of the game Carry Back, his opponent in many races, caused a lady to send a cable which read:–

"Dear C.B. Today is your final debut–I love you so much and it hurts me to think that I will never see you in the winner's circle again–but you are the Champ, Kelso or no Kelso–please stay smart utterly and on top as you have been–I will never forget you, my adored hero–with all my love–(signed) Joan Frederickson."

Many hardened racegoers must admit to something approaching tears at those moments when a really great horse is greeted by thunderous applause on his return in triumph to the unsaddling enclosure. Such a horse was Ireland's magnificent steeplechaser Arkle, whose fan mail was sometimes addressed–and was not delayed in transit–"Arkle, Ireland".

It is said that the presence of an outstanding horse who so dominates the betting that he starts at ridiculous odds inhibits the racegoer from attending, but crowds have never been bigger than those which went to see Arkle in his races in England, and at Sandown Park he was applauded on his way to the start and when he passed the stands first time round. Anyone who was around the winners' enclosure when Arkle stepped into it after galloping home at long odds–on witnessed a moment of high emotion, perhaps unexpected by those who regard the frequenters of race tracks as entirely mercenary and unlikely to get excited about anything except a good-priced winner carrying their money. Arkle's owner, Anne, Duchess of Westminster, admitted to being more owned by Arkle than vice-versa and when receiving the trophy for the National Hunt Champion, which was presented in London for the first time in 1966, said, "I do wish Arkle was here to receive this award instead of me–he does do things so well."

There are memories too, not only of racehorses in the peak of training, but of great veterans in retirement. Armed, once the world's leading money winning gelding until Kelso came along, was dozing under a row of chestnut trees on Calumet Farm, Kentucky, not dreaming of the time when the crowd roared as the commentator called his name, but just glad to be allowed to move around at his own pace these days. Summertime, New Zealand's champion stallion many times over, his coat gleaming and looking a picture of health as he showed off to a crowd of visitors, was nevertheless completely blind and relied on his great friend and companion, a Jack Russell terrier, who stood beside him, cocking his head on one side and gazing intently at the big horse as if trying to divine his thoughts. Owen Tudor, in the evening of his life, gentle and game to the last, nuzzling the coat-sleeve of the stud groom who had brought him into the world twenty-eight years before at Lady Macdonald-Buchanan's Newmarket stud, his dark brown coat flecked with white, and as soft as a kitten's to the touch.

There was a time when horses kept their feet firmly on the ground, except when galloping flat out for their master's pleasure and profit. Today they are hurried about the world by jet and prop, and have shown themselves the most adaptable of travellers at speeds far in excess of those that they can achieve on a dirt or turf course. We have

stood apprehensively at airports and waited for a trailer to disgorge a trembling racehorse, as jets roar off into the night in quick succession, and marvelled at the way that half a ton of horse has taken a quick look round at the airport lights, climbed the ramp into the waiting freighter, looked startled at the noise of engines at take off and then settled down to doze over mid-Atlantic. People who handle these world wide travellers have developed an expertise unknown 25 years ago, have come to know the likes and dislikes of their regular passengers–"just hold her head up at take-off, she'll be all right"; "Forget about him, he knows more about this trip than the control tower"; "Watch that one, he got hold of my arm at Deauville and didn't let go until we'd climbed to 3,000 feet, I swear it."

Flying round the world with horses demands immense patience, a knowledge of the best bed and breakfast joints in many places, and little family life. We recall in his late sixties Collis Montgomery, tall ex-steeplechase rider who had travelled horses to many countries for a firm of international shippers. His wrinkled face creased into a smile as he told of the antics of the Queen Mother's horse Gay Record, who was hell to all who had anything to do with him, but whom Monty reformed with gentle riding every day and with the occasional day's hunting. Between his trips in charge of famous stallions, mares and potentially famous foals, Monty would revisit Gay Record at his stables, taking with him presents of apples and carrots. He was tragically killed when a cargo plane carrying eight mares developed a fault on landing at London Airport and crashed in flames.

Poles apart from Monty in this racing world of many characters is little Jock, the man who seldom bought a railway ticket and whose solemn duty is to try to find winners for those who come to the races unequipped with such information, providing that they invest a certain sum for little Jock as well. Jock has travelled thousands of miles on British Railways gratis. Sometimes he feels obliged to buy a ticket to a station just down the line to ease his task of getting on to the platform, but 300 miles further on you can see him leaving the train with all the assurance of a well respected traveller. But usually he has no ticket at all, and it was on just such a day that he was caught sitting in the restaurant car playing a quiet game of cards with three men who looked intelligent enough to know better, when a ticket inspector walked in at each end of the car simultaneously. Jock demonstrated complete control of the situation. He was wearing a dark suit, similar to those of the restaurant car crew. He quietly stood up, draped a napkin over his arm, picked up a basket of bread rolls and walked out to safety. Arcaro, Piggott, Breasley, Gordon Richards, and Longden may have shown exceptional calm while waiting for that opening on the rails or timing their challenge to the split second, but they never matched such cool resourcefulness as this.

Of such is the world of racing made up, the courageous and the crooked, the sentimental and the tough, the expert and the optimist. Racing is colour and noise, sweat, dust, beer and betting, fear, bravado and cold professional brilliance, with all the while the people are watching the horses and begging them to do the right thing. Let us take a look round this world, and enjoy some of the people, the horses and the courses, that make up the whole lively scene.

The Most Important Ingredient

The most important ingredient in horse racing around the world is still the horse. In modern racing, it can be argued that the public and their money are the more important. Housed in a comfortable stadium, it is said, the fans would probably be quite happy to bet on electrically propelled horses, the result of each race being decided by an impartial computer housed in the basement of the grand stand.

The nearest approach to this soulless means of parting a man from his money was when English racing was hit by severe weather in 1967. A London evening newspaper hired computer time to stage "races" for well known steeplechasers, feeding in information about their capabilities and the nature of the course over which they were supposed to be racing. Bookmakers offered betting facilities on these mythical races; the computer churned out a list of the order in which the horses were supposed to be running at various stages of the race; and a commentary was broadcast. But the whole performance left most people with a hollow feeling that racing was being made to look ridiculous.

Around the horse has grown up a vast industry which today is linked all over the world by the ever increasing exchange of blood lines. But what extremes of capital investment and size of projects there are within that industry. At one end of the scale there are vast stud farms with miles of white fencing and neatly painted barns, and at the other end, the solitary brood mare kept in the back yard of a small inn, or getting her grazing in a field hired from a local farmer.

Racing and breeding, on whatever scale they are tackled, are based on hopes and dreams, and require above all patience. From the time when the decision is taken to breed a thoroughbred to the time when he first sets foot on a racecourse as a two-year-old, can be anything up to four years. In the case of a late maturing horse, it may be decided not to run him until the Spring of his three-year-old season, so that the owner has another six months of sitting by his fireside dreaming of that moment when, as he hopes, the outcome of his investment some four and a half years ago defeats the opposition in one of the classic trial races and becomes favourite for the Derby.

Most owners start by buying a yearling at one of the major sales. This method cuts down the time they have to wait before they see their money in action on the racecourse, and they let someone else bear all the worry of the breeding stage of the operation. But for real pleasure of what is anyway a most wonderful feeling–to stand in the winner's enclosure after seeing your horse gallop to victory–nothing can beat having been the breeder as well as the owner of that horse who now, with heaving lungs, tightened muscles, veins sharply pencilled in beneath the skin, is at last rewarding you for all the scheming and waiting.

The story usually starts, in the Northern Hemisphere, at a sale such as Tattersalls Autumn Sales or the December Sales at Newmarket, or the Fall Sales held at Keeneland in Kentucky, where you can either buy a mare who is already carrying a foal, or perhaps invest in a filly three years old whose breeding and racecourse performances suggest that she has the characteristics needed to produce whatever you have set your mind on–a Derby winner, a top class middle distance horse, a champion sprinter (at this stage there is no point in thinking in terms of mediocrity; championship material is what you are aiming for). North of the Equator all horses have their birthday on January 1, whatever date they were actually born on, so that the whole generation moves from one age group to the next at the same time, thus simplifying the definition of a two-year-old, a three-year-old, and so on for racing purposes. In the Southern Hemisphere, the date is July 1, so it is at the mixed sales at Trentham, New Zealand or in Sydney, Australia, or in Buenos Aires, Argentina, in March and April that you buy your filly out of training.

Next there is the question of the choice of the stallion with whom your filly, or mare as she will be called when she becomes a four-year-old, will be mated. The small breeder has to face the fact that in these days of syndication of the best horses, it is difficult to obtain a "nomination" to the top class horses, and also very expensive. It just depends on your pocket. Sir Ivor, the winner of the 1968 Epsom Derby, went to stud in Ireland at a record fee for Europe of £8,400, and was immediately fully booked at that price, while in America you have to pay 20,000 dollars to send a mare to champion racehorse and sire of champions Ribot.

But below the very top, there is a large body of good class sires at reasonable prices from which to choose, using your own judgement and not being influenced by the trends and fashions which tend to sway the breeding world, but looking for a stallion of good conformation, good performance, a high fertility figure and a good or promising record at stud.

It is easy enough to lay down the rules like this without being financially involved, but in practice the hazards of breeding are countless. For instance, there have been many examples of full brothers or full sisters to brilliant horses proving quite useless. The mating of the same sire and the same mare that had previously produced a champion has on the second occasion resulted in something which was not fast enough to win a ploughing match. The Seventh Earl of Derby once said that the only thing to do was to breed the best to the best and hope for the best. He might have said "breed to the best one can afford."

Three factors govern the start of the breeding season in the Northern and Southern Hemispheres. It would be fatal for a horse to be born in the Northern Hemisphere before January 1, as he would then immediately become a yearling on New Year's Day and would, at least until he was much older, be competing on unequal terms with horses born the right side of January 1. The other factors are that the period of gestation for a mare is 48 weeks, or 11 months, and that a mare can be some 15 days early in foaling, so that to ensure as far as possible that the planned foal is not produced before January 1, stallions do not start covering their mares until February 15. In the Southern Hemisphere, the breeding season starts on August 15.

Mares carrying foals from last year's covering, usually start arriving at the stud farm where the stallion stands before or soon after Christmas in the Northern Hemisphere and stay there until they are considered safely in foal, 42 days after the last occasion on which they were covered by the stallion.

Life on a stud farm during the foaling and breeding season is as hectic as any job in the world. Stud managers, grooms, veterinary surgeons are on duty for almost the whole of 24 hours, snatching sleep when they can.

Unfortunately for those involved, most mares give birth between 6 p.m. and 6 a.m., and during the rest of the day the ordinary routine of the stud farm must go on. Mares who have already foaled have to be covered by stallions, stalls cleaned out, animals fed and watered. On a big farm such as the National Stud at Newmarket, where four stallions stand, or Mr Arthur (Bull) Hancock's Claiborne Farm in Kentucky, where there are usually some 25 stallions every season covering 40 mares as many as 30 foals may be born every 24 hours during the hours of darkness.

Our theoretical filly, who becomes a four-year-old mare on January, will on average have to be covered two or three times by the stallion chosen for her before she is found to be in foal and then she will go off to either the owner's home farm while the foal inside her develops, or be boarded out at around £12 a week in Europe or 40 dollars a week in America.

During the Autumn, the owner has to make up his mind which stallion the mare is going to visit when she has produced the foal she is now carrying. This is when one may suddenly realise the cost of the whole business. If all goes well, and the mare produces a foal in each of her first two years, at the end of three years you will have a mare, a yearling ready to go into training at about £2,000 or 5,000 dollars a year, and a foal. All of them eat, are prone to illness, need blacksmiths to look after their feet, expensive horse boxes to move them around the country. You may not have had a runner in a race yet, but you probably have a bank manager whose interest in the cost of keeping thoroughbreds is increasing every day.

So your mare goes off to the next stallion of your choice, with luck produces her foal safely, and is mated with another stallion to start the cycle all over again. We say with luck, because a certain amount of this is necessary in breeding as well as racing. The fact is that in spite of the big advances which have been made in the veterinary field in recent years, diseases and accidents result in more than 40 per cent of matings not resulting in a foal which reaches the racecourse. Mares prove barren, or have miscarriages, give birth to dead twins, or animals with malformed limbs. There are many things that can go wrong between the time you take that decision to breed a Derby winner and the time when your young hopeful goes into training.

But let us assume that all goes well and that early in March, 16 or 17 months after you bought the mare, she produces an awkward, gangling, spindly-legged object, hardly capable of standing up and for the first 24 hours at least always likely to collapse in a heap in the straw under the light of the infra-red lamp switched on in the box to give him or her added warmth in the early days of his life.

As he gains strength, he will be led out each day with his mother and turned out in a paddock with other mares and foals, gradually learning to nibble grass and eventually in the Autumn being weaned from his mother's milk and switching over to hay, grass, oats and bran mashes.

For the foal the next 12 months after the mare has gone off to her next assignation, will be spent in the company of other youngsters, all of them assuming the title of yearling on January 1, and all of them learning the rough and tumble of life in a boarding school. One of the most alarming sights is to see half a dozen yearlings, worth anything between £250 and five figures, being turned loose in a paddock in the morning, galloping flat out to the far railings and then sweeping round in a wide arc, or pulling up suddenly in a corner

"Bridling, saddling, breaking and training" by T. Smith

almost shoulder to shoulder. Their exhilaration at being out in the open has given many a stud manager some anxious moments as they let off steam, and occasionally things do go wrong. The manager of a studfarm on the outskirts of Newmarket recalls two valuable yearlings colliding head on in a disastrous morning spree which resulted in both of them being so badly injured that they had to be put down.

By the Autumn of his second year in this world, our yearling will probably be slightly more sober and in August or September he will be sent either to the sales, if he is being bred for commercial purposes, or straight into training to learn the job of work that is his *raison d'être:* how to gallop from A to B faster than any of his rivals.

Until now it is unlikely that he has had any piece of equipment on him other than a head collar to facilitate leading him to and from his barn and the paddocks, but now must start the gentle business of getting him used to the feel of a metal bit in his mouth, reins on his neck, a saddle on his back and eventually the weight of a human being in the saddle weighing upwards of 84 pounds.

Methods of breaking and making a racehorse vary enormously all over the world, but one thing is certain–that this is the most vital stage of a horse's career. Impatience or harsh words or a blow at this stage can produce a horse who is sour or unmanageable for the rest of his racing life.

Once the yearling has been ridden by a stable lad he is ready to go on to the next stage–learning how to gallop, sometimes singly, sometimes in company with other youngsters, and at gradually increasing speeds.

Life starts in earnest much earlier for an American yearling than it does, for instance, for his counterpart in England or France. Prize money is available at tracks in Florida and California from January 1 when he becomes a two-year-old, and by that time many youngsters will have been working at fast speeds on training tracks and will be ready by the start of the year to begin earning their keep. In most European countries, two-year-olds seldom run before March and if a horse is a classic prospect, he may not appear until towards the end of his first season, giving him every chance to develop and strengthen before he is asked to race at full speed.

Essential experience for two-year-olds in almost every major racing country around the world today is that of starting stalls. One outspoken old lady from England who accompanied a tour of American racecourses in the days before starting stalls were introduced in England came stumping back from a courtesy visit to the starting gate at Laurel saying "Damned little boxes. No self-respecting horse should allow himself to be put into those rabbit hutches." She had sadly, but perhaps happily for her peace of mind, passed on by the time that stalls were introduced on English courses and there, horses, like their American cousins, had to learn at an early stage of their training how to walk in and out of practice sets of stalls which were established at training centres all over the country.

The fact is that a sport which relies so heavily on the betting public for its income has a duty to see that backers are given a good run for their money. The all-seeing eye of the television camera had been showing people just how bad many of the starts from the old-fashioned barriers were, with well-backed horses often facing in the wrong direction when the tapes went up.

One of the fascinations of a new racing season is to see the young two-year-olds coming to the course for the first time, fresh-eyed and curious, taking a keen interest in everything going on around them, walking around the parade ring, looking out over the heads of spectators at the sights of the racecourses. Older horses who have run in many races may plod round the ring looking almost asleep, but for the youngsters that first visit to the racecourse gives new meaning to a life which may already have settled into a routine of work in less exciting surroundings.

Few jockeys would touch a two-year-old with his whip in his very first race for fear of leaving a permanent impression of fear and pain right at the outset of the horse's career, and it is not generally realised by the public how little whips are actually used on the horse. Many of the best Australian, English and American jockeys wave it backwards and forwards alongside the horse rather than hit him.

Some horses need very little encouragement to get them to race to the limits of their ability. One such was Colonist II, the first horse owned by England's wartime leader Sir Winston Churchill. Colonist II had all the dogged determination of his owner, and bitterly resented it if another horse tried to overtake him. Winner of 13 races, he would grind his teeth and stick his neck out if another horse tried to pass him once he had taken the lead. On one occasion in the middle of a race his jockey Tommy Gosling recalls that Colonist II screwed his head round and tried to bite a rival who was challenging him.

Would that all horses had such determination. Unfortunately constant racing, perhaps harsh treatment, or sometimes an inner ailment which the horse is not capable of telling his trainer about, but which may cause him pain when he is racing, may earn a horse the reputation of being a rogue. Often such horses appear wearing blinkers, which

"Broodmares with their foals" by T. Smith (top); "Famous horses of the Duke of York" by James Seymour, in the collection of the Queen Mother (centre) and The Flying Dutchman, the 13th Earl of Eglinton's Derby and St. Leger winner in 1853, painted by John Frederick Herring, senior.

aid their concentration on the job in hand. Old-fashioned trainers used to use blinkers in a manner which one does not hear of so much these days. Before fitting them to the horse for the first time, they would take him to the gallops, give him a thorough beating with a whip known as a Long Tom, put the blinkers on him and then have him galloped fast. The theory was that the first time the horse had blinkers put on him on the race-course, he would recall his previous experience and would gallop as fast as he could in the race. Though methods have changed considerably, many people still find it profitable to back horses wearing blinkers for the first time, as it is then that this equipment often has its greatest effect on the performance of the horse.

By the time a horse has had a couple of races as a three-year-old he should be showing his owner whether or not there is the slightest point in going on paying his training bills after this season. A horse who is too slow to earn his living on the flat, may find a ready buyer among the jumping trainers, providing he has sound legs and the build to cope with the obstacles, and the Autumn mixed sales, where the whole story may have started five years earlier with the purchase of that three-year-old filly out of training, give the sadder, wiser and poorer owner an opportunity of ridding himself of the expensive four-legged friend. The facts of life are that in a typical year in England, 1961, there were 4,800 horses that ran in flat races, and there were 2,600 races, so that allowing for those horses which won several races, there were many more which did not get a share of the prize money.

For the fortunate man who has bred for himself or bought a really good horse, the pleasure of standing in the winner's enclosure is enhanced by the knowledge that in the case of a filly, she becomes of great value for the stud, and in the case of a colt, besides his capacity to win more races, he becomes an even more valuable asset as a stallion prospect.

World wide increases in prize money as major racing countries have closed down or limited the activities of bookmakers have, over the past forty years, steadily driven bloodstock values up. A measure of the increase is shown by the price of 640,000 dollars which was paid by a syndicate of Kentucky breeders when the 1952 Epsom Derby winner Tulyar was sold by the Irish National Stud in 1955. Thirteen years later, Vaguely Noble, winner of the Prix de l'Arc de Triomphe against brilliant international competition at Longchamp, was syndicated to stand at stud, also in Kentucky, for five million dollars. The current world record for a stallion is held by Nijinsky at $5,440,000.

So there are the two sides of the coin. The horse, the most vital thing in the whole world of racing, can cost you plenty–and many owners have been watching their colours carried on race-courses for years without ever knowing the thrill of owning a winner. Or he can put you in the big money and in these days of international competition, take you to the famous racecourses of the world.

Breeding farm at Chino, California, owned by Mormon Rex C. Ellsworth, seen above handling two-day-old foal. The 440-acre farm has more than 100 broodmares and a five and a half furlong training track.

32   Freedom—at Argentina's leading stud, Haras Comalal

Saddled and ridden for the first time, Chino, California

A cooling touch after training at San Isidro, Argentina

38   "Just do it like you know how, baby"—Churchill Downs, 1970

The Strength of French Racing

On Sunday mornings all over France, men and women sit at café tables with three essentials in front of them–an aperitif or a coffee, a newspaper and a tiercé betting form. In this pleasant habit of meeting over a small drink to discuss the racing prospects and place tiercé bets with the owner of the café, who acts as an agent for the pari mutuel, lies the strength of French racing. The tiercé demands that you place in correct order the first three horses in the big race of the day, and if you achieve this you are in line for a big prize. Backers all over the world cannot resist the attraction of such a proposition–big money for a small outlay–even if what they are required to do is fantastically difficult if reflected upon in a quiet moment. In one year the French bet some £275 million on the tiercé alone. Some 70 per cent of that is paid out to winners, £55 million goes to the Government, and £36 million goes to French racing for the improvement of courses, for prize money, and for the general benefit of the racing industry. It has reluctantly been acknowledged by other European racing countries that in the past 10 years, France has pulled her way to the front in international racing by intelligent planning and by sheer weight of money.

The controlling body which has been responsible for the progress of French racing, and in particular of Longchamp, home of the world's greatest international event, the Prix de l'Arc de Triomphe, is that which possesses as long a name as any similiar organisation in the world–the Societé d'Encouragement pour l'Amelioration des Races de Chevaux en France. It has been encouraging and ameliorating French racing since 1833, but never more actively than in the years since World War II. When it was first formed, the Société controlled, in conjunction with the Stud Administration, a rough sort of racecourse in the Champ de Mars in Paris, between the Military Academy and the banks of the Seine. Champ de Mars, now the site of the Eiffel Tower, was opened in 1806, the year in which French racing became organised with the blessing of Napoleon, but the Stewards of the Société were not at all happy with their course and in a report to the Committee referred to the dangers likely for the runners in a coming big race becuase of "the terrain's shortcomings and the whirlwind of pebbles and dust."

The Société had already established a racecourse at Chantilly and ran the Prix du Jockey Club (French Derby), for the first time there in 1836, but Chantilly, attractive though it was and is, lies 32 miles from Paris. Then in 1856, two years after the City of Paris had acquired the Bois de Boulogne on its outskirts, the Société were given permission to create a racecourse. This involved building, at their own expense, a grandstand and laying out a course on the plain of Longchamp. This was a large clear space in the Bois, dominated at one end by the windmill which still stands at the end of the racecourse.

On April 27, 1857, Parisians made, for the first time, the Sunday migration out to Longchamp for an afternoon's racing–12,000 of them, driving in 700 carriages, riding on 250 hacks, or walking on their own two feet. Racing took place on seven days at Longchamp that year–now there are 40 days racing a year.

There have been bad moments in the history of Longchamp. The course was devastated in the war with Prussia of 1870 and afterwards the old stands had to be patched up and enlarged. New grandstands were inaugurated in 1904. And in 1906 the crowd, enraged by a bad start, burnt down the wooden pari-mutuel buildings. These were replaced by cement buildings, which later housed the selling machinery of the automatic totalisator, installed in 1928 by an Australian company.

By 1914, France could claim that Longchamp was the most beautiful racecourse in the world and that the Grand Prix de Paris, a stern test for three-year-olds over 1m. 7f. in July, was the world's richest race. But during World War I Longchamp became first a grazing ground for cattle and then a combined airfield and American ambulance centre. Racing re-started in 1920, and in 1934 the course was equipped for floodlit racing, which went on until World War II. Paris social life was then at its grandest and to go to dinner and night racing at Longchamp, with the men in silk top hats and tails and the women in their finest clothes, was very much one of the things to do. The "Nuit de Longchamp" was one outstanding night every year from 1934 up to the outbreak of war, with dining tents, dancing floors, orchestras and music hall turns.

Racing was suspended in France in September, 1939, but started again in 1940 and went on right up to the time of the invasion of Paris. Many high class stallions and mares were "acquired" by the Germans for nominal payments and, in all, French breeding was deprived of some 700 thoroughbred horses, which went to Germany and Hungary. But towards the end of 1940 the head of the German Military Occupation in Paris announced that there were no objections to the renewal of racing, and in spite of severe rationing of fodder, French racing carried on through the war on a limited scale. Thousands of bicycles replaced automobiles in the Longchamp car parks, and racing continued there until a tragic day in April 1943 when German anti-aircraft guns fired on a formation of Allied planes just as the horses were going to the post for the first race. Bombs were dropped, seven people were killed and the Germans ordered the closing of the racecourse. The fixtures were thereafter divided between nearby Le Tremblay and Maisons-Laffitte, although about a year later racing was allowed to resume at Longchamp.

French breeding had severe set-backs when more than 20 studs in the great breeding area of Normandy were destroyed during the Allied invasions. Some of the horses confiscated during the war were returned from Germany in 1945 including the outstanding stallions Brantome and Pharis, but in general French racing set out on its period of recovery after the war in a considerably weakened state, which makes even more remarkable the progress that it has made in the past 20 years.

There is so much international racing these days that one tends to think that it is an invention of the years since World War II, but races like the Grand Prix de Paris and the Ascot Gold Cup attracted foreign challengers almost from their inception. The Grand Prix was won by the English Duke of Beaufort's Ceylon in 1866, only two years after the race was first run, while the list of winners includes Major Eric Loder's Spearmint, in 1906, Mr J. Watson's Lemonora in 1921, both from England, and Signor Federico Tesio's Italian champion Nearco in 1938.

In 1920, the Société took a selling race, called the Prix de l'Arc de Triomphe, and turned it into a valuable test for three-year-olds against older horses, at weight-for-age, open to runners from all countries. An English horse, Comrade, won it in the first year, and while this grandson of the Grand Prix winner Spearmint never made his name at stud, the list of Prix de l'Arc de Triomphe winners since that day includes many horses and mares which have influenced racing and breeding throughout the world.

Thus, as French racing got into its stride again in 1946, it had a pre-war tradition of international competition to look back on, and two men, M. Marcel Boussac and the present Director-General of the Société, ex-civil servant and racing journalist Jean Romanet, have had the full support of Société members in their drive to make the international theme predominant in modern French racing. Boussac and Romanet realised probably earlier than anyone the possibilities opened up by the transportation of racehorses by plane. The first flight for racehorses to England was in a Bristol aircraft operated by Boussac in October 1947, which plugged its way over the English Channel

to Blackbushe Aerodrome in Berkshire carrying three horses, two of which, Arbar and Djelal, won at Ascot before returning two days later to France. Since then thousands of horses every year have been flown on the England-Ireland-France circuit.

By 1956 French horses had won America's Washington D.C. International twice–Worden II in 1953 and Master Boing in 1956–and that year, M. Boussac and his colleagues were delighted to hear that two American horses would be crossing the Atlantic to run in the Prix de l'Arc de Triomphe. Mr C.V. Whitney's Fisherman, winner of the Washington D.C. International the previous year finished ninth at Longchamp, but the same owner's Career Boy ran a fine race to finish fourth behind the brilliant Italian horse Ribot. There were in fact six foreign contestants in a field of 14, drawn from France, Italy, America, Ireland and England, setting the pattern for future Prix de l'Arc de Triomphe.

Money talks in every language, and today, with French prize money increasing every year, the franc has become the most important unit of currency in the racing world. Breeders and owners from many countries have realised that in France they have a far better chance of breaking even with their horses than in their own countries. Americans, Germans, English and Irish owners are sending their horses to race in France or to be trained there. At any of the major French courses, the breeding of the runners on the racecard presents a glittering array of blood from half a dozen countries. On Prix de l'Arc de Triomphe day in 1967, 44 out of 96 runners in the six races were bred outside France; every runner in the sprint event was sired in England, Ireland or America.

And what of the French racegoer–how does he view all this? Fervently patriotic and insular in the past, he has come to recognise the styles of Australian and English riders, contrasting with the more lively riding of the French jockeys. There was a time when the top English jockeys did not exactly look forward to riding in France–they could expect fairly rough treatment from the French jockeys–but today they are in and out of the jockeys' changing rooms at the major French tracks every few days. Familiarity plus the all-seeing eye of the camera patrol has settled things down. The French punters still tend to overestimate the chance of a locally-trained horse ridden by their idol Yves Saint-Martin and to allow a foreign horse to start at too long a price, but gradually they have become more knowledgeable about important races in other European countries.

On a quiet day at Longchamp, the vast, magnificent stands, prefabricated and rolled into place in 1965, when they were slotted into the stone-built towers which characterised the old stands, are far too big for the job.

But on a big race day, Longchamp is crammed with people, betting, eating, drinking, looking at fashions, shouting abuse at jockeys beaten on favourites or cheering them half an hour later for winning. Down in front of the stands in the second enclosure a crowd gathers round two men arguing with alarming ferocity whether or not a jockey was doing his best on a certain horse, while gendarmes watch dispassionately just in case the discussion gets out of hand. In the private enclosure around the glass-walled weighing room where jockeys can be seen as if in a gold-fish bowl, climbing onto the weighing machine with their saddles on their knees and caps pushed back on their heads. Members of the French racing establishment wearing grey bowlers or "melons noirs" (black bowlers) or on classic days top hats and tailcoats, shake hands with each other and with the members of foreign Jockey Clubs, blood-stock agents and journalists. Standing in the slow-moving tote queues you can see the horses in the parade ring on the colour television sets suspended above the parimutuel windows, or if there is time you can stand on the big range of steps which give a superb view of the parade ring. It is only a few years since there was no proper parade ring at Longchamp. The horses moved round an ill-defined circle, on the inside of which were hundreds of racegoers sitting on chairs fanning themselves with the flimsy racecards that French courses favour. It was easy to blunder into the path of a sweating, eye-rolling favourite worried by the proximity of so many people or to feel the wind of a lashed-out hoof. Today thousands of people can stand on the steps in safety and see the horses parade, incidentally giving the lie to an old theory, probably put about by the English, that it is only the English racegoer who really likes to *look* at the horses. We suspect that if American racegoers were given more opportunity, instead of having parade rings tucked away in inaccessible places, they too would take the opportunity of getting to know the horses before the race.

On big days the infield at Longchamp teams with humanity who have paid a franc to come in. The whole course is 1 m. 6 f. around, though loops at the top end of the course enable a variety of distances to be achieved from the same starting point. The Prix de l'Arc de Triomphe field starts in front of the old mill, races away behind a clump of trees (–"au petit bois l'ordre est..." says the commentator), round the widest of the loops, down a slight hill and into the straight, with some three furlongs to race to the winning

Transportation, wartime style, Longchamp, 1942. In the background the bronze statue of Gladiateur, the French-trained winner of the English Triple Crown, 1865. Bottom: Poster by Cassandre for the Prix de l'Arc de Triomphe sweepstake, 1935—one of the rare occasions when a famous artist lent his talent to the promotion of racing.

From top to bottom:
The Prix du Jockey Club at
Chantilly, 1846
Longchamp racecourse soon
after its opening in 1854
The Grand Steeplechase de Paris,
1846
The racecourse at Croix
de Berny

post from a final bend where there are often some hard luck stories. The top jockeys reckon you have to be in the first seven or eight at the bend to win the Arc, but a few winners have come flying up from further back, as those in front have wilted on the gruelling run-in of well watered turf.

Two other racing Sociétés have courses in the vicinity of Paris, but work closely with the Société d'Encouragement in all matters of rules, policy and fixtures. The Société de Sport de France was until 1967 responsible for the racecourse at Le Tremblay, now being replaced by a new course under construction at Evry, while they also control the Bellerive course at Vichy. The Société Sportive d'Encouragement controls Saint Cloud, with its fine modern stands put up in 1954 and its hedge-lined parade ring. This is a somewhat sharp race-course favouring the horse with a good turn of speed, but its Grand Prix de Saint-Cloud in July always attracts a high class field, including over-seas challengers. The Societé Sportive also owns the course at Maisons-Laffitte, a long narrow track on the banks of the Seine where a lot of bread-and-butter racing takes place. Maisons-Laffitte is probably unique in having four different winning posts spread out over six furlongs, which makes it extra exciting for the backer who thinks his horse was beaten on the post and then realises the race is still on.

On only six days a year the magnificent race-course at Chantilly springs to life. More than 3,000 horses are trained in the area so there is never any shortage of runners, but Parisians still prefer to patronise the racecourses on their doosteps instead of driving 45 kilometres out to Chantilly. Here the French Derby takes place early in June and grey toppers are the order of the day for "the nobs", and again a week later on French Oaks day. The forest of Chantilly comes right up to the perimeter of the course, and trees and hedges surround the saddling area and the parade ring. Over on the far side of the course the horses race past a large ornate building, erected in 1735, which was the stables of Chantilly castle.

Chantilly is one of the great training centres of the world, with magnificent stables put up by the great owners who train in France, such as the Aga Khan, M. Marcel Boussac and the Rothschilds. There is a school and hostel for apprentices. An immense variety of training grounds, on sand, on turf, over fences and hurdles, surround the town. Through the forest there are more than 30 miles of gallops and rides, so that a horse can have different training ground and scenery every day for a month. The Société maintain a fleet of vehicles to rake the sand rides twice a day, special traffic lights are installed to get the training strings across the main road that runs through the town, and everything possible is done to help the thoroughbred horse and those who look after him.

The same short men wearing caps and breeches that you see walking down the High Street at Newmarket or riding their bicycles to stables are there in Chantilly. You see them buying their racing papers in the main street or sitting in the bar of the Hotel Sylvie talking racing. Chantilly is full of stable lads with English sounding names, descendants of lads who came to work for rich American and French owners earlier in the century or stayed on in France after World War I. There is a sort of pigeon French racing language which makes it fairly simple for the English lad staying over with horses in France to enquire where he can get hay or water or where the six furlongs gallop starts or where to find a beer or a bit of skirt after he has fed his horse.

Racing goes on at the main Paris tracks from late February until early December with the exception of the month of August, when the scene is transposed to Deauville, the Normandy seaside town which like most seaside towns seems barely alive in the winter. Big wooden shutters cover the windows of the Hotel Normandie, the Casino and many of the shops, sand blows on to the road on the sea front. But in the summer the harbour is full of big yachts. The Paris fashion shops open up local branches, Mercedes and flash sports cars are in every street. The racecourse, with its half-timbered weighing room, is close to the centre of the town and there is flat racing three or four days a week, interspersed with jumping and moderate-class flat racing at Clairefontaine just down the road. Deauville also has its polo and its yearling sales. Almost the entire staff of the Société d'Encouragement move down from their Paris headquarters with their families and conduct their business for a month from Deauville. The prices in the town are at their worst for the month of the races and while it is pleasant to have a change of scene it is also pleasant to get out of Deauville before the local traders have the shirt off your back.

During the winter, Deauville seldom sees a racehorse, though one February on a visit to Chantilly we found that an appallingly hard winter had made preparation of candidates for the early French and English classics impossible there and several of the leading trainers had vanned their horses out of the area of snow and frost down to Deauville. In brilliant morning sunshine small strings of Chantilly thoroughbreds enjoyed exercise on the beach, their breath blowing white in the cold air.

Deauville is surrounded by France's richest breeding area. Just outside the town at the village of Touques, through which the summer traffic jams heading for the beach stretch at the weekends, is the Baron Edouard de Rothschild's Haras de Meautry, home of the small but brilliant Prix de l'Arc de Triomphe winner Exbury. Within 50 miles or so there are some 150 stud farms from the very large, like Meautry with its magnificent chateau nearby, to little places where sheep and goats stand around in the yard but the thoroughbreds are well fed and capable of earning a good price at the sales and a slice of that rich French prize money afterwards.

Longchamp, Saint-Cloud, Maisons-Laffitte, Le Tremblay, Chantilly, Deauville and Vichy–these are the names of the tracks which hand out the bulk of the money, and one talks about France having centralised racing. Top class racing is centralised, but further down the scale there is enjoyable sport during the winter at Cagnes-sur-Mer in the South of France, and quite a few of the fashionable trainers (who may have more than 200 horses in their stables) are not above sending a small contingent of horses down to pick up some of the smaller prizes. Then there is racing at Bordeaux and Lyon and Poitiers, Paray-le-Monial, Maure-de-Bretagne and Sille-le-Guillaume. There are, in fact, nearly 360 racecourses in France, some holding only one meeting a year on a local holiday, others half a dozen, but all drawing something for prize money from the central fund. These little meetings may not have the camera patrol, starting stalls or the photo finish, tramps probably sleep under the stands for most of the year and the local farmers graze their cattle on the course, but it is horse racing and it keeps alive the interest that prompts the Frenchman to bet and keep the whole pot boiling.

Contrast of British Racing

A mid June afternoon at Royal Ascot: soundlessly up the wide green course a cavalcade approaches. Redcoated outriders on grey horses are followed by open landaus drawn by more grey horses, their white tails swishing. Inside the first carriage is Queen Elizabeth II, beautifully and formally dressed, gently waving in response to the cheers from thousands of men holding grey top hats and women with flower-garden hats lining the rails.

Yet this may well be the Queen's second appearance of the day on the green turf of Ascot. Often in the early morning, wearing head-scarf, hacking jacket and jodphurs, she likes to ride over from near-by Windsor Castle with some of the younger members of her house party, and they will put on an informal, private race up the testing straight and past the famous winning post on this, her own racecourse.

Contrast is the spice of British racing.

At Chester, racing is watched by crowds standing on the ancient city walls, looking down on the flat oval space beside the River Dee called the Roodeye, where the Romans are said to have raced their horses.

At Newmarket, the horses gallop across wide sweeps of open downland, where the larks are singing.

Towcester, with its thatched weighing room, is set in a cup of woods in the green English Midlands.

Pontefract in Yorkshire is the miners' course. Pitheads and coal tips frame the far end of the racecourse.

At Stratford-on-Avon you can see the lineal descendants of Shakespeare's youthful companions jostling on the rails to watch the jumping.

At Windsor, a course held in the arm of the Thames, you can cover the half mile from the town Riverside station to the races by boat.

In fact the delight of British racing is its variety. Each of the sixty-three British racecourses (two of them at Newmarket) has its individuality. Many of the older courses are on common land, where the first horse races were matches between noblemen and gentry for high stakes. The horses were ridden by tiny lads, some of whom weighed scarcely more than three stones (42 lbs). The lads were put into simple colours so that they could be distinguished at a distance, often the colour of the owner's coach being chosen. So originated the complex, strictly controlled system of racing colours, of which seven thousand different sets are registered in Britain.

Later, many park courses were built, which were enclosed by a wall and on private ground, so that admission could be charged to all parts of the course.

No two British race tracks are the same. Twenty-four courses are right-handed, like Ascot. Thirty-eight are left-handed, like Epsom and Doncaster. Two—Windsor and Fontwell—describe figures of eight. The turns are different, the slopes are different, the turf is different. At several courses, such as Kempton Park near London and Haydock Park in Lancashire the tight, weedless turf has been cared for but not turned by the plough for two thousand years. The straights are of varying lengths, some finishes are uphill, some downhill and some level. Trainers and jockeys—and punters too—have to be expert at finding the right course, the right tactics for each horse. It makes for interesting racing.

Because racing in Britain is on turf, race meetings are of only a few days duration, so that the courses are not cut up by the horses too much. Because Britain is a comparatively small country a trainer can take a horse from Perth in the north even to Devon and Exeter in the west. In practice trainers generally concentrate on courses fairly near at hand, though the widening network of motorways is making transit easier. There is no necessity to have training barns at the racecourses themselves. The racecourse stables are only used during the race-meeting, or perhaps for a night or two beforehand in the case of horses who have come from Ireland or France.

Trainers keep their horses in their own yards at home. Some eleven thousand racehorses are in training in Britain, and there are four hundred licensed trainers, mostly grouped around Newmarket, headquarters of British racing, Lambourn in Berkshire, or Epsom and in several centres in Yorkshire. Each trainer has between a handful and eighty horses in his yard.

In addition some hundreds of "permit trainers" are allowed to train horses for themselves and their families, but not to take in horses to train for other owners.

Every year in Britain, on the fifty six English and six Scottish racecourses, plus one on the borders of Wales, there are about eight hundred and fifty days of racing allocated by the Jockey Club.

Flat racing opened traditionally with the Lincolnshire Handicap, which used to be run at windswept Lincoln in the third week of March, and closed with the Manchester November Handicap at Manchester in the first days of November. But both Lincoln and Manchester racecourses

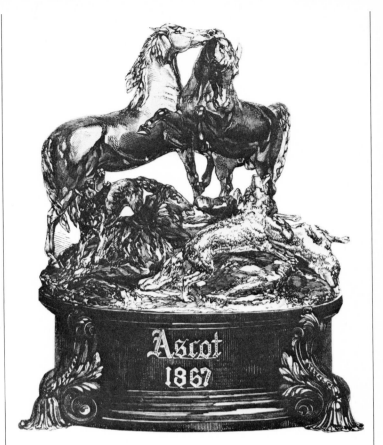

have closed down in recent years. Races perpetuating their names are now run at Doncaster at the start and towards the finish of each season. Doncaster can be as cold as Lincoln was in March but at least it is run with more business acumen than was the Lincolnshire course, and it now has a handsome modern stand with an allweather betting hall housing both tote and bookmakers.

The jumping season opens on the first of August, and steeplechasing and hurdling continue until mid June in the following year.

Of England's five classic flat races the One Thousand Guineas at Newmarket and the Oaks at Epsom are for fillies only, and the Two Thousand Guineas, the Derby and the St.Leger at Doncaster are open to both colts and fillies.

Newmarket, home of the Guineas, is the headquarters of British racing. Situated partly in Cambridgeshire and partly in Suffolk some seventy miles from London, the town had for two centuries its principal raison d'être in horseracing, though now light industries have moved in. To the visitor it seems that Newmarket is a town of tiny men, so many ex-jockeys and stable lads are employed as station porters, street-cleaners, barmen and shop assistants. The Jockey Club's imposing Georgian red brick headquarters dominate the High Street, and everywhere you look are bootmakers, saddlers, sales paddocks, horseboxes, photographers of horses, and men poring over *The Sporting Life*, the daily racing paper.

In Newmarket are concentrated some thirty five racing stables and almost two thousand horses in training, forty studs, the Tattersalls sales paddocks where horses change hands for more than eleven million pounds a year, many of them going to three dozen overseas countries, the Equine Research station of the Animal Health Trust, which includes the Forensic Laboratory where scientific dope-testing and research are carried out, and the new National Stud.

Of vital importance to Newmarket are the two big areas of training grounds owned by the Jockey Club, which spread east and west of the town. Almost the whole year round these training grounds present a wonderful picture to the horse-lover in the early morning, as the strings of horses leave their yards to train on whichever gallops are opened on that particular day, as listed on a noticeboard outside the Jockey Club office.

Newmarket, which was then a thinly populated area, was discovered as a sporting centre by King James and became a horseracing centre through his grandson, Charles II in the 1660s. Charles II loved to watch the gallops of Warren Hill, and as the winds blow cold over the downs, he had a little shelter built for him, first of wood and later of stone. He used to bring his court with him to Newmarket, and although a small palace was built for him, many of the senior officers of state could find no lodging but had to sleep in tents: Newmarket was not all that popular with the older courtiers.

Charles II had a hack called Rowley, from which he took his own nickname of Old Rowley, and Newmarket's two Classics, the Two Thousand and the One Thousand Guineas, are fittingly run over the Rowley Mile.

Charles II enjoyed race-riding himself. He twice won the Newmarket Town Plate, which is still run each Autumn, though not under Jockey Club rules, for which part of the nominal prize are some of the delicious spicey sausages which are made in the town.

The Newmarket Town Plate is the only flat-race in Britain in which women are eligible to ride, and they take full advantage of it.

We would probably have the greatest difficulty in understanding a conversation held in Tudor or Stuart English, so much has pronunciation changed. Charles II would not be the only one who would have difficulty in understanding the conversation that goes on to-day in betting enclosures on Newmarket Heath or on any of England's racecourses.

The tic-tac men have developed a language which has its origins in many sources–rhyming slang, Yiddish, prison phrases, the tic-tacs' own semaphore. They know the faces of owners, trainers, big bettors. They lean forward to try to catch the size of the bet and the name of the horse when "a face" comes up to back a horse with one of the big bookmakers. They place bets themselves for their own bookmakers or offer to lay a horse at slightly better odds than the ruling market price. The pace is furious, the conversation incomprehensible.

"Any carpet the second fav?"

"Demmy, Demmy–too late he's laid it."

"Who wants a one ten to eighty?"

"You're joking, it's half arm with Hill."

"What's it bar?"

"Bottle."

"Put me fifty this one on the nanny."

"Neves to rofe the splonk now, each of two."

All this is child's play to characters with names straight out of Damon Runyon–Mickey Fingers, Big George, Sheffield Ike, Sammy the Barking Seal–but we had better explain: that carpet is three to one; the second fav is the second shortest price horse in the betting; Demmy is a bookmaker; a tic-tac is offering to lay anyone £110 to £80 the favourite; but someone points out that bookmaker Hill is offering the longer price of six to four (half arm derives from the tic-tac signal for this price, with the right hand making a chopping motion across the joint of the left arm);

someone else wants to know what price they are offering bar the favourite, i.e. the price of the second favourite; bottle is rhyming slang for two (bottle of glue–two); a bookmaker tells his runner to bet £50 for him on the tote (nanny goat); and now the market has changed so that two horses are joint favourites at seven to four (neves is back slang for seven, rofe an anagram of four, and splonk is–no one knows why–tic-tac word for the field.

Epsom, home of the Derby and the Oaks, is some fifteen miles south west of London on the edge of the Banstead Downs. It became famous early in the seventeenth century because of the medicinal properties of its salts. Self-indulgent gentry, staying there for the cure, amused themselves by watching horse races, as well as cudgelling and wrestling matches and other sports of the day, on the Downs.

The horse races became established when the gay reign of Charles II replaced the dour regime of the Puritans, but it was not until the 1780s that the Derby, the race which has given its name to the championship event for three-year-olds in many countries, took form. The twelfth Earl of Derby, a very lively young gentleman, came of age in 1773 and took over the lease of his uncle's house near Epsom, which was called The Oaks. That uncle incidentally was General Burgoyne, an illegitimate son of Lord Bingley, who commanded the British army in the American War of Independence and surrendered at Saratoga in 1777.

The pleasure-loving young Earl of Derby always acted as a steward at Epsom races, which then consisted entirely of heats for older horses run over two or four miles. In 1779 he and his friends introduced a new race for three-year-old fillies over one and a half miles, on similar lines to Doncaster's St. Leger, which had recently been founded. The race, named the Oaks after the house, was a success, and so the next year the Derby for three-year-old colts and fillies was first run over a distance of one mile, which was increased to the present one and a half miles in 1784.

The Epsom Derby is now held in the end of May or at the beginning of June. It is a great English occasion, and people who never follow horse-racing feel that they must, almost in duty bound, bet on the Derby. Six fillies have won the English Derby (four of them also won the Oaks), four grey horses, thirty two horses with names beginning with the letter S, but none starting with Q, X, or Z. The shortest named Derby winners are Pan (1808) and Sam (1818), the longest The Flying Dutchman (1849). The smallest horse to win the race was Little Wonder (1840), who stood only fourteen hands three and a half inches. Unlikeliest winner was perhaps Sunstar (1911), who was lame shortly before the race, dead lame when he pulled up and never ran again. Only one owner has won both Derby and Grand National in the one year, King Edward VII (then Prince of Wales) in 1900: he also won two other Derbys.

Mrs. ("take two dozen eggs") Beeton of cook-book fame was born in the Epsom grandstand. Her father was manager of the racecourse and the family lived in a house built into the old grand-stand.

The present Derby course, first used in 1872, bends first uphill to the right, and then after about four furlongs commences a long left-hand turn through 180°, at the same time sloping quite steeply down to Tattenham Corner, which leads to a straight of about half a mile.

On Derby Day, the Hill, the free part of the course, swarms with people. Open-topped omnibuses drive down from London and park in a long line beside the inner rail, while the occupants open champagne bottles and picnic hampers, or mingle with the crowd to place their bets. Gypsies, sellers of candy-floss, tipsters, men with placards forecasting doom, bookmakers shouting the odds–and above it all the music from the electric organ in the fairground where the stately wooden horses on the roundabout go up and down, round and round, with unseeing eyes as the field for the Derby flashes by.

For the jockey with a fancied ride in the Derby it is not just another race, however hard he may try to make it so:–

Time to leave the weighing room, you can hear the fairground music, ... into the car with other jockeys to drive down to the paddock, at least it's the only course where I have a ride–Huge field, good looking lot this year. There's my owner and trainer. "Afternoon madam, sir. Yes, I understand, don't show him in front too soon, I'll make my run when we're a furlong and a half into the straight." *(Hope he's good enough.)* "Thank you, madam, do our best."

Interminable preliminaries, mounting, the cool leather of the saddle through the thin breeches, parading, cantering down... now the long walk across the downs to the start. He's settling down nicely, not sweating up, the crowds don't seem to... whoops! Hell, what was that? Would you believe it, that woman's tried to pull a hair out of his tail!

Tightening girths... shall I get off and rest him? No, hardly worth it. Calling the roll. "Here, Sir." *The French colt's playing up. That Prendergast chestnut is a real beaut. I hope I don't see him in front at the distance.*

"Even numbers into the stalls, jockeys."

In he goes, quiet as a lamb. Not like at Lingfield.

Reared up. That sweaty French colt is hanging about at the back. Get the bastard in, my fellow's getting fed up. Here we go, the last one's in. Let'em go, Sir. Now. A yell. We're off. Steady lad, steady. Drop him in sixth or seventh on the right-hand rail. Uphill here. A lot of bumping—we took that one. But he's not lost his stride.

Now steadily across the course to get a place on the left-hand rail for that mad rush down the hill. They're going too fast in front. Try for a place on the rails behind the Irish horse. Bit too far back, but not too bad. Down, down towards Tattenham Corner. The bad horses are beginning to roll about and come back. Damn their owners, who want to see their colours in the lead SOMEWHERE.

The French horse is not coming down the hill too well, he's dropping back, but the Prendergast horse is improving. Can I get through behind him? No … no … YES.

Into the straight in fourth position, that Major Portion horse is still leading, but I don't think he'll stay … I think he'll roll out, I'll take a chance and come inside him–Now. Now we're second to Prendergast. Hell, that French colt's at my knee.

Coming to the last furlong …. the Frenchman's dropping back. But the chestnut's still full of running, holding on … no, he's coming back, he's coming back. Give my lad one good one now, ride him out with hand and heel. He's game, he's finding a bit, he's doing it, doing it … half a length, a neck, four strides to go … we've done it, we've WON!

There has never been a Derby without drama. But if ever there was a bitter-sweet Derby it was in 1953, Coronation year. The Queen had her good Aureole in the race, which took place in the same week as her coronation. Opposing him was Pinza, who was owned by Sir Victor Sassoon. Now Pinza had been bred by one of the greatest, if not the most placid of English trainers, Fred Darling, a superb judge of a horse who had trained eighteen classic winners, including seven winners of the Derby. Fred Darling had sold Pinza as a yearling because his own health had failed, and now he lay dying at his beloved Beckhampton on the Wiltshire Downs. Only his will to see Pinza win the Derby kept him alive, that and a letter he had received from the Queen, wishing him a return to health and hoping that if any horse were to beat Aureole in the Derby, it would be the colt he bred.

Riding Pinza was the popular champion jockey Gordon Richards, who had ridden in twenty seven Derbys and never once been on the winner. He had just been knighted by the Queen in the coronation honours, the first and only jockey to be so distinguished. There were twenty five more runners, but these two, Aureole and Pinza, were the ones the public had taken to their hearts, and as it

"The last horse race run before Charles the Second of Blessed Memory" near Windsor Castle, August 24, 1684, drawn by Francis Barlow, (top); and S. Begg's drawing of the scene after Persimmon had won the Epsom Derby of 1896 for the Prince of Wales (later King Edward VII), who is leading in the winner.

happened, these were the horses concerned with the finish.

Round Tattenham Corner, Gordon Richards on Pinza was second, several lengths behind Shikampur. Aureole was sixth. Two furlongs out Pinza took the lead, and opened up a considerable advantage. The bright chestnut Aureole, his white legs flashing, chased him, but he had too much to do, and passed the post four lengths behind Pinza.

What a wonderful reception Gordon Richards got as he rode into the unsaddling enclosure, and he valued equally the warm congratulations he received from the Queen, who sent for him a few minutes later. Fred Darling listened on the radio to Pinza's triumph. He lived long enough to hear from Gordon Richards, who had long ridden for him, the story of the race, and three days after the Derby he died.

The racing man loves a great filly, and since the war there have been several that were specially admired, among them the gallant Meld, winner of the One Thousand Guineas, Oaks and St. Leger, the last of these when she was sickening for the cough and was discovered afterwards to have a high temperature; and that lovely mover, the grey Petite Etoile (now almost pure white at stud) unbeaten in six races at the age of three, eventually passing Meld's record-winning total for a filly. Since then the Duke of Devonshire's gallant Park Top has pushed the record even higher.

When Charlottown, Meld's son by Charlottesvill, ran in the 1966 Derby some backed him out of affection for his dam, others warned, quoting the old adage that an Oaks winner seldom produces a Derby winner—and indeed only five have done so in nearly two hundred years.

Once again the trainer early associated with the Derby colt did not prepare him for the big race. The late "Towser" Gosden, who trained at Lewes and who had never won the Derby, had to give up training on doctor's orders after he had had Lady Zia Wernher's Charlottown as an unbeaten two-year-old of classic breeding. He passed Charlottown on to the care of young Gordon Smyth, formerly private trainer to the Duke and Duchess of Norfolk, and in his first season as a public trainer.

Charlottown did not appear under the best auspices in the spring. Foot trouble took him out of one race, and in his pre-Derby race in the Lingfield Derby Trial he seemed to wage a private war with Ron Hutchinson, the able Australian who just could not get on terms with him, although Charlottown, when he did get going, was catching the winner, Black Prince II, at the rate of knots.

So Ron Hutchinson was stood down, and wily old Scobie Breasley, the grandfather, the man with the master pounce, was put up in his stead. In the paddock Charlottown was sweating up and then—to trainer Gordon Smyth's horror—as the moment for jockeys to mount came, Charlottown trod with his near fore on his off fore foot and left his new racing plate shining on the turf. Charlottown's hooves had given trouble all through the winter, and had hardly grown at all. There was hardly any horn into which to re-fix the nails. Gordon Smyth had brought his skilled blacksmith George Windless with him, and cigarette in mouth, watched by millions on television and waited for by thousands on the course, the smith imperturbably refixed the plate.

Scobie, who always likes to be last out of the paddock anyway, unconcernedly took a leg up, and fifteen minutes late the Derby runners left for their walk across the downs and late start. Incredibly, being plated, far from fussing Charlottown, seemed almost to have calmed him down.

The race itself saw a duel between the oldest and the youngest riders in the field as young Paul Cook, aged twenty and only a few weeks out of his apprenticeship, rode out Pretendre, the much fancied English colt, in a thrilling duel against the wily Australian on his thin-hooved Charlottown. Charlottown prevailed by the measure of a neck, the smallest winning margin since the French Lavandin beat Montaval ten years before. "Towser" Gosden, happily, was well enough to greet Charlottown in the winner's enclosure.

In the third week of June comes Royal Ascot. Ascot, about thirty miles west of London, is royal in fact as well as name. The first races were held here in 1711 after Queen Anne, who was too stout to ride, but hunted in her light, two-wheeled carriage, at a furious pace, enjoyed a gallop on the heath there and decided it would make a fine racecourse.

To-day Ascot is administered by the Ascot Authority, headed by the Queen's Representative, the Duke of Norfolk. The Duke is England's premier duke and hereditary Earl Marshal (his appointment at Ascot is not hereditary). He is an outstanding organiser, and was responsible for the arrangements at such major national events as the coronation of Queen Elizabeth, the state funeral of Sir Winston Churchill, and the investiture of the Prince of Wales and he has long been involved in the running of British racing. The Ascot Authority is a non-profit-making body, and all profits are ploughed back into racecourse improvements.

Fantastically, until after World War II, Ascot had only four days' racing annually, and the stands stood silent for the rest of the year. These four days of Royal Ascot are still one of the world's great social occasions, but twenty five

From top to bottom:
The "Black Ascot" of 1910
when the country was in mourn-
ing for King Edward VII.
Lord Derby welcomes back his
Epsom Oaks winner of 1927,
Beam ridden by Tommy Weston.
The Royal Stand at Ascot,
about 1843

days' racing are now staged each year. Big new stands have been built, and steeplechase and hurdle courses have been added, and turfed with grass from Hurst Park, a popular London course given over to building.

Ascot fashions are famous. There are always some eye-catchers, hats as wide as carriage wheels, loaded with an aviary of birds. Thousands of elegant women escorted by men in grey toppers and morning suits are seen to good effect against the magnificent trees and the fastidiously groomed green turf. "The mourning Ascot", after King Edward's death, when every woman wore black or white or grey was picked by Cecil Beaton for the race scene in "My Fair Lady" (although in the stage version poetic licence allowed the horses to race the wrong way round).

Ascot racing is as outstanding as the hats. Of the many great horses seen at Ascot in recent years, the author remembers cycling to the course early on several mornings to watch the famous Italian horse Ribot do his preparatory gallops for the King George VI and Queen Elizabeth Stakes, held at the July meeting over one and a half miles.

At 6.30 a.m. on the day that Ribot did his final fast work there was one small solitary figure in the paddock at Ascot, awaiting the appearance of the great horse. It was the famous Australian golfer Norman von Nida, who had climbed a fence to get in.

"Where is everyone?" he asked. "If this was Australia and a horse like Ribot was going to do a gallop, there would be thousands of people watching."

As the early sun began to warm the backs of the little group of groundsmen, reporters and ardent racing fans who had assembled, Ribot came out, led by his constant gallops companion Magistris, a useful winner in his own right. Ribot's final gallop, only two days before the event, was over the full distance of the big race, to the amazement of the spectators, used to the more cautious training methods of England.

Magistris set off in front with Ribot, who was ridden by veteran jockey Enrico Camici, going easily behind him. Four furlongs from home, although Magistris was doing all within his power, Ribot coasted by in overdrive, and left Magistris three parts of a furlong behind him at the winning post. Ribot's time for this training gallop was within two fifths of a second of the course record, and the horse looked ready to go round again. His time for the gallop was actually faster than that which he clocked on the day of the race, for by then it had rained and Ribot had to contend with something he had never encountered in his sun-drenched homeland–mud.

The race itself was watched by the Queen and

members of her family. The runners included the Belgian champion Todrai, and horses from France, Ireland and England, among them the Queen's game and consistent High Veldt. Todrai added drama by suddenly charging the starting tapes, sweeping his jockey off on them, and galloping away free. He went half-way round the course, turned and charged back. The starter, seeing the danger, lifted the tapes and Todrai galloped through the waiting group of horses, round to the stands and turned into the paddock, where he was caught and returned to the start.

After all this Todrai actually led into Ascot's gruelling uphill two and half furlongs straight, with Ribot close behind him. Todrai swung wide towards the stands, and the crowd roared as they saw the royal colours of scarlet and purple with black cap on High Veldt slip through on the rails. But Ribot's jockey had his horse perfectly balanced and headed for better going which he had discovered when walking the course. In the straight Ribot was under pressure for probably the first time in his career, but he lengthened his stride and sailed on to beat the royal horse by five lengths.

Ribot was one of the all-time champions, and he had it in him to pass a spark of his brilliance on to his progeny, who have won top-class races under a wide variety of conditions in America, Italy, France, Ireland, England and Germany.

Glorious Goodwood, which is almost as fashionable as Royal Ascot, if more intimate a race meeting, takes place at the end of July, on the lovely wooded estate of the Duke of Richmond and Gordon on the Sussex Downs some sixty miles south-west of London.

Goodwood racecourse was laid out in 1801. Among the outstanding horses who have been seen at Goodwood are St. Simon and the famous unbeaten Hungarian mare Kincsem, who ran in and won the Goodwood Cup of 1878.

The great St. Simon, bred by Prince Batthyany, who died before the horse had been seen on a racecourse, was afterwards bought by the Duke of Portland. The rule was then that nominations made by a dead owner were void (this rule was challenged by thriller writer Edgar Wallace, in a friendly action against the Jockey Club, and since 1929 nominations stand, even if the owner has died). So St. Simon lost his classic engagements and was seen for the first time in a minor race at Goodwood.

York is another superb racecourse, just outside a walled city which retains a great deal of the best of what is old. But there is nothing old about the stands on Knavesmire, which also house a racing museum. There can be seen the unexpected sight of a pair of scarlet braces (known in America as suspenders) lovingly cross-stitched with flowers by a Duchess for a jockey with whom she was in love. The Duchess was the famous or notorious Duchess of Montrose, a fiery woman of terrific personality, who raced under the pseudonym of "Mr Manton", the jockey Fred Archer, who won 2,748 races before he took his own life in a fit of depression caused by dieting, at the early age of twenty nine.

A modern jockey who had to retire from the saddle because his health was being undermined by wasting, Harry Carr, who was the Queen's jockey for many years, said of York's August meeting that it was "the finest days' racing of the season in my opinion."

Yorkshire racing has always a specially enjoyable atmosphere. There is no man who enjoys a day's racing, a good horse or a good bet more than the Yorkshireman. Large crowds watch the St. Leger, run at Doncaster, one hundred and fifty six miles from London and just over the Lincolnshire border into Yorkshire. The St. Leger is the oldest and longest of the classics, run over one mile six furlongs and one hundred and thirty two yards.

Named after Lieutenant-General St. Leger, it was first run in 1776. The famous animal painter Herring chanced to arrive in Doncaster on St. Leger day, and was so impressed by the excitement, the movement, and the vivid colours of the silks, that he decided to become a painter of racehorses, although first he had a spell as driver of a four-in-hand coach, which is perhaps why there is such a sense of participation in his paintings of horses.

It is at Doncaster that the winner of the Two Thousand Guineas and Derby can set the seal of the St Leger on his success, and so become one of the select band of triple crown winners. Only twelve horses have won the full triple crown, not counting wartime substitute races. The first winner was West Australian (1853), bred and owned by a kinsman of Queen Elizabeth the Queen Mother, John Bowes; followed by the French bred Gladiateur (1865); Lord Lyon (1866); Ormonde (1886); Common (1891); Isinglass (1893); Galtee More (1897); Flying Fox (1899); Diamond Jubilee (1900); Rock Sand (1903); Bahram (1935); and most recently Nijinsky (1970).

It might seem the pleasantest dream in the world to have such a horse in your stable, but let the case of Diamond Jubilee, who won the triple crown for the Prince of Wales, afterwards King Edward VII, speak for itself.

Diamond Jubilee was by the great St. Simon out of a wonderful but jadish dam Perdita II, and own brother to Persimmon, who had won the Derby and St. Leger of 1896. Consequently he was made a great fuss of at Sandringham, where he was bred, and was a spoiled child of a horse, rebellious and peevish if he did not get his own way, but at bottom honest and gallant. He was a big bright bay horse with dark legs and a dark line down the middle of his back, of whom his trainer Richard Marsh said "He had a most intelligent head and a perfect back and loins."

On Diamond Jubilee's first racecourse appearance, as a two-year-old at Epsom, his trainer was just remarking on his perfect temperament when the horse lashed out and kicked a man on the hand. He then went on to give a dreadful display at the starting post, walking about on his hind legs and generally behaving disgracefully. His jockey, Jack Watts, a taciturn man who was troubled by wasting, said afterwards that the colt had tried to get a jockey's foot in his teeth. At the next appearance at Newmarket he threw Watts. "It may be that the colt had an intense dislike of Watts," wrote Richard Marsh "but it was as nothing compared with the jockey's dislike of the horse."

Morny Cannon was then given the ride on Diamond Jubilee and got on rather better with him, but in the colt's early three-year-old days Cannon, after riding him at exercise, jumped off Diamond, as he was called in the stable, whereupon the horse seized him in his teeth and flung him to the ground. Help was at hand, but Cannon later excused himself from riding Diamond Jubilee in the Two Thousand Guineas.

Who to put up? None of the leading riders was both available and willing. But in the stable Diamond Jubilee would do anything for his work rider, Herbert Jones, a plucky, cheery man who was an excellent breaker and horseman. Richard Marsh asked if he could put the work jockey up on the horse in the Two Thousand Guineas, and the Prince of Wales at once agreed.

The professional backers mistrusted Jones and the horse was allowed to start at eleven to four against in a field of ten. He easily won the Two Thousand Guineas, and although–at the special wish of the Prince of Wales–he even paraded, which was not then compulsory, before the Derby of 1900, he won that race too without undue stress.

The St. Leger was something else again. Richard Marsh recounted in his memoirs, "He was in one of his really devilish moods, and intended giving everyone a fright with the greatest impartiality. Really, I never thought I should get a saddle on him … a rare old battle we had in a corner of the paddock which I generally used for saddling my horses at Doncaster … Every time I went near him with the saddle he would shoot straight up in the air, and stand on his hind legs. This went on to such an extent that time was getting short. He

broke out in a heavy sweat, and I know I did."

Then a further performance was in store when Jones came to get up. The colt was thoroughly roused, and would have nothing to do with being mounted, until Jones took him unawares and sprang on to his shoulders. In an instant he had got into the saddle, but if he had not been an acrobat as well as a horseman he would certainly have been shot off. Up went the colt and when he came down Jones found his irons and all was well.

Diamond Jubilee, starting at odds of seven to two on, duly won the St. Leger from the second favourite Elopement, ridden by Morny Cannon.

Although there is no sixth classic at Doncaster for fillies, the Park Hill Stakes, named after the house of General St. Leger, is often regarded as the staying three-year-old fillies' championship.

It was at Doncaster that we encountered a bookmaker who told us an extraordinary story of mutual trust between himself and one of his clients, a man who farmed large areas in the east of England and who bet in thousands of pounds at a time. The farmer telephoned the bookmaker's office just after the last race one day and said he had intended to have several bets during that afternoon but had been busy on the farm and had not had time to get to the phone. He did not know any results. Could he place some bets now?

Knowing that the farmer seldom put less than one thousand pounds on a horse, the bookmaker took a courageous decision and agreed. The result was that the farmer backed four horses for a total of £8,000, had one winner and on balance lost £3,500 on races which had already been run. Thereafter he often used to phone after a busy day, and the bookmaker told us:

"It was hell sometimes when he started to read out his bets–£2,000 on this, £4,000 on that, when you knew the horses had already won. One afternoon he took £24,000 off me, but I knew who I was dealing with, and of course I paid him out. On one occasion he had runners at two meetings and in the paddock at one of them his trainer congratulated him on his horse having won at the other meeting. He was furious with him. 'Now I can't back the animal!' he roared, and the trainer never made that mistake again."

Just as the spring is enlivened by the great spring double on the Lincoln and the Grand National, so in the autumn the betting man is seeking to find the winners of two great handicaps run at Newmarket at different meetings in October, the Cesarewitch Stakes, a handicap for three-year-olds and upwards, over two miles and a quarter; and the Cambridgeshire Stakes, also for three-year-olds and upwards, over one mile and one furlong. It is a great sight to see the finish of these races, which normally attract large fields, as they sweep uphill towards the finish on the Rowley Mile.

So the flat-racing season draws towards its close. The horses begin to turn in their coats, the better-known performers are let down and roughed off for the winter, while vast fields of less successful horses strive to make a late contribution towards their training bills.

In the sales paddocks, the yearlings come under the hammer as the eternal optimists, owners and trainers, search for the horses to carry their hopes past the following season's winning posts.

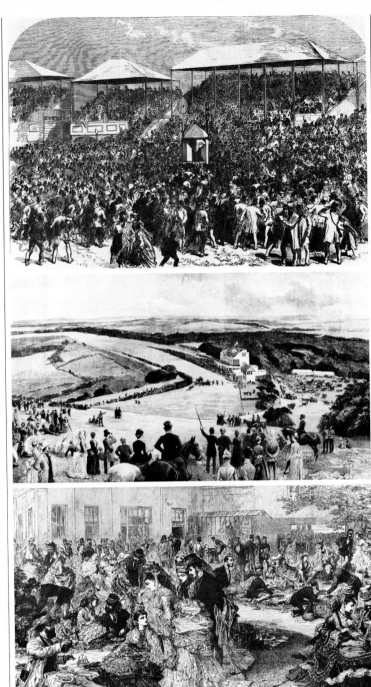

From top to bottom:
Derby Day, Epsom, in the 1860's.
Goodwood, 1886. Today's view from Trundle Hill includes a much longer range of stands and a parade ring on the right in the area used here for parking horse-drawn vehicles.
Picnic scenes behind the stands at the Royal Ascot meeting.

Racing in Ireland– Part of Life

Horse racing in Ireland is not just part of the entertainment industry. It is an integral part of life, and a vital factor in the nation's economy. That is just one reason why an Irishman becomes explosive when an Englishman refers to a horse which may have won one of Europe's classic races as being British bred, when in fact it was foaled in Ireland.

True, if you look at a map of Europe, Ireland is designated as being part of the British Isles, but try arguing that one out with an Irishman. Ireland is Ireland, and in the late 1960's, the export of horses was worth over £6 m. to the country. Any attempt to lump Ireland in with England, Scotland and Wales is doomed from the start.

Conscious of the fact that they have something to sell, Irish breeders and the racing industry as a whole are far more aggressive in their publicity than their rather complacent counterparts in England. This is big business, and they are not prepared to sit around and watch the English whittle away lumps of credit for horses which they think should be assigned to Ireland's number one export.

In practice, the boundaries between French-bred, English-bred, Irish-bred are becoming almost impossible to define. A big breeder like the late Major Lionel Holliday, for instance, may have had a mare covered by a stallion in Ireland, returned her to his stud in Yorkshire to foal, and sent the weanling back to Ireland to thrive on the limestone land of County Meath, while the mare was later flown to France to visit a stallion of American parentage.

But Irish racing has hauled itself up by its boot-straps in the past twenty years in a way which does credit to those concerned with the sport, and which has enabled it to take its place on the European circuit both as an effective competitor for the prizes of other countries and an attractor of high class horses for its best races.

Even allowing for the decrease in the value of money, the £33,000 for some 440 races each year in the 1850–77 era compared to the £780,067 given in 1968 for 1,092 races shows the way in which Irish racing has grown. With tote turnover reaching a record £4,064,170 in 1969, there is every reason to believe that this figure will continue upwards. Perhaps a comparison with the 1850 figures does not best reflect the growth of Irish racing. More realistic is the fact that in 1948 the prize money totalled only £269,222. In 1969 it was £959,163.

In 1949, when this growth was just under way, an Irish writer attributed the progress that was being made to three things–the Tote, the declaration of runners the day before racing, and the levy of $2\frac{1}{2}$ per cent on backers' stakes on the racecourse.

Ireland, with its wide range of courses, from the Curragh to the little country meetings like Sligo and the beach meeting at Laytown, where two hours after the last race the sea has come in to wipe out the hoof prints of the runners, does not operate a tote monopoly, but at least there is a healthy income for racing from both on- and off-course betting on the tote, and it is growing all the time.

Overnight declarations, enabling the off-course backer to know the runners the day before racing, were introduced in Ireland many years before they were in England, because the Irish authorities realised the publicity value of this move. Unfortunately they did not back up the move by demanding that a horse should be declared for one particular race, and a horse could be down to run in as many as four events on one day, but it was a step in the right direction.

Irish-bred horses were making their mark in the races of France and England well back in the 19th century. Brownstown Stud, owned by the McGrath family and the place at which the 1969 Prix de l'Arc de Triomphe winner Levmoss was bred, was in existence before 1800, and may well be the oldest stud with an unbroken history in the British Isles. The stud bred Birdcatcher, who was twice leading stallion in Great Britain and Ireland, in 1852 and 1856, and who passed on his ability to many good horses. Levmoss is in fact one of his descendants.

Brownstown is in County Kildare on the edge of the wide stretch of land which is virtually the heart of Irish racing–The Curragh. This huge plain of nearly 5,000 acres, surrounded by training stables and stud farms, is the scene of Ireland's classic races, and a good many more activities besides. A delightful and informative press release made at the time the Irish Sweeps organisation boosted the Derby from being a race worth only £7,921 in 1961 to over £50,000 in 1962, said that "it would be no exaggeration to state that all the undermentioned events could take place on the Curragh simultaneously and perhaps with little or no interference with each other:- a military review; troops shooting at the rifle range; trainers' strings at exercise; a race meeting with the car parks occupied; the Kildare Hounds drawing a covert for a fox; the Naas Harriers scenting furze clumps for a hare; a coursing meeting; a prize fight".

There is also an 18 hole golf course, a hospital supported by the Irish Sweepstakes organisation, and military barracks. The release continued "Driving through the Curragh at night, one can be startled at several points by the challenge "Halt! Who goes there?" To the answer "Friend" the sentry will speed you on with 'Pass Friend and Good Luck'. At the extremity of the plains can be heard the crack of rifle practise at the butts" (presumably by floodlight).

The Curragh has many historical associations, not only with horse racing. On the north side is Donnelly's Hollow, where in December 1815 Dan Donnelly beat George Cooper, the gipsy from England, in a famous bare-fist prize fight, watched by thousands from the high banks surrounding a natural amphitheatre.

The Curragh was the headquarters of the British Army up until the end of The Trouble in May, 1922. In those days, many of the British officers followed the local hounds, and rode in point-to-point races and at the nearby Punchestown course. On the departure of the British, the Irish Army took over the Curragh military establishment, continued hunting with local packs and to go racing at The Curragh. A major reconstruction of the racecourse stands took place during this era, and further extensions were needed to cope with the large crowds which were expected for the first running of the Irish Sweeps Derby on the last day of June, 1962.

Irish racing went into this expensive venture with a thoroughness which was admirable, and the list of horses which won the race, or contested it in the first eight years of its running shows that the gamble of trying to put it on the map as one of the most important three-year-old races in Europe has succeeded.

The first year, 627 yearlings from 15 different countries were entered for the Derby. On the day before the race, Dublin was teeming with "the international set" owners, members of Jockey Clubs from America, France and England, journalists from the States, New Zealand, Australia, Germany, France and England, television camera teams from half a dozen countries.

Besides doubling the accommodation in the stands, the Irish Sweeps Derby Co-Ordinating Committee fully appreciated the importance of giving the press every facility and built behind the stands a large communications block with ample desks and phone facilities for a press corps far greater than any that had ever been seen at The Curragh. Car parking facilities were vast, and the police and military co-operated in devising a one-way traffic scheme which worked so efficiently that one detected a feeling of surprise among the organisers themselves.

And the race itself immediately stepped into the international field when Tambourine II, owned by Mr and Mrs. Howell E. Jackson and bred at their Bull Run Stud in Virginia, ridden by Roger Poincelet and trained by Etienne Pollet at Chantilly, won by a short head from the fast-finishing Irish horse Arctic Storm. American owners were also responsible for the third and fourth horses, with Mr Townsend B. Martin's Sebring in third place, and Mr Raymond Guest's Epsom Derby winner Larkspur fourth.

The author thumbed a lift the following morning on the Bristol freighter plane which lumbered its way back to France carrying Tambourine, in order to reach St. Cloud in time to see Match (later to win the Washington D.C. International in America) defeat a high class field for the Grand Prix de Saint Cloud. International racing was very much the theme of an exciting week-end, and Irish racing journalists set the seal on it by asking the writer to carry to St. Cloud a racing print, the back of which bore their signatures, to be presented to Roger Poincelet in the weighing room at the French course.

Irish racing and breeding has progressed steadily in the past decade. In 1962 the 1,000 Guineas, and 2,000 Guineas, both run at The Curragh, were worth only £3,356 and £5,585. In 1969 they had risen to £8,065 and £9,866, while, thanks to sponsorship by the firm which produces that other valuable Irish export, Guinness, the Irish Oaks has been increased in value from £5,030 to more than £20,000.

Leading trainers such as Vincent O'Brien, who first made his mark as a trainer of jumpers (he won the Aintree Grand National three years running with Early Mist, Royal Tan and Quare Times), and the hard-working, hard-playing ever optimistic Paddy Prendergast, train for more and more American owners, many of whom have purchased stud farms in Eire or keep brood mares there.

Racing in Ireland has variety and charm—a local school band thumping away between races at Leopardstown, the Laytown meeting on the beach, where the time of the first race is dictated by the tide; the chat in the bars at country meetings such as Killarney and Tuam.

But Ireland is also an aggressive competitor in the international field where both racing and breeding are concerned. Probably some 3,000 horses are flown between England and Ireland every year, and there is increasing traffic between America and Ireland, with more and more good stallions going to stud in the Emerald Isle.

Installed, by degrees, at Longchamp

Topyo wins the 1967 Prix de l'Arc de Triomphe for Mme. Suzy Voltera, beating Salvo

An even break at Longchamp

What will win the next? For rich and poor the problem is the same—unless you are worrying about whether that woman over there is wearing the same hat as your own.

Chantilly, home of the French Derby and training centre for many of Europe's best horses

The final, vital hundred metres to the winning post

Royal Ascot—to see and to be seen

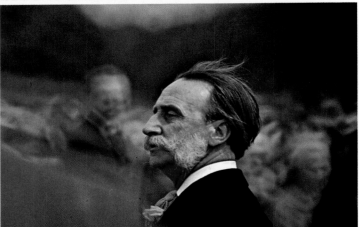

An empty racecourse is a sad
place. It's horses and people that
make it live—punters, newspaper sellers, bookmakers, ladies
of fashion, jockeys and tipsters
and officials.

Epsom, home of the English
Derby, where the noise of the
fairground and the cries of the
hot gospellers mingle with running commentary on England's
greatest race.

The Queen and Prince Philip
arrive at the Royal Ascot meeting (top) driving up the straight
mile course (bottom), where the
width of the course often results
in the field dividing into two
quite seperate groups.
Page at right:
Epsom would not be Epsom
without the admonitions.

Poised at Ascot for the final drive to the post

Germany–An Ability to Produce Good Horses

The story of German racing since World War II has been one of a long uphill battle, first to overcome the financial problems of a nation shattered by the greatest conflagration the world has seen, and then to try to achieve a place in the front line of international racing and breeding. The first part of the struggle had been achieved by 1956, the second part continues.

The golden era of German racing was undoubtedly before the First World War, when Hoppegarten, now in the Eastern Zone of Berlin, had much the same atmosphere as did Chantilly in France at that period, with many English trainers, jockeys, and stablemen mingling with the local horsemen. Jockeys like Australian Frank Bullock and Fred Winter, senior (who rode Cherimoya to victory in the English Oaks when he was only 17) and trainer Reg Day, who in 1971 was still managing studs in Newmarket at the age of 88, were very much part of the scene. Reg Day, in fact, established a record as a trainer which gives some indication of the strength of the German racing industry at that time. Invited to go to Germany in 1906 to take the Graditz stables of the Kaiser Wilhelm II, he transformed a fading and out-of-luck establishment into one of the most successful in the history of the country. The £40,000-plus he won in stakes in 1912 was more than any other trainer in the world.

After the First World War, German racing took longer to recover than it did after the inferno that Hitler initiated in 1939, but some good horses were seen on German courses in the intervening years. Undoubtedly the best of these was Oleander, a racing machine, who recovered from a broken pelvis as a two-year-old, after he had won his first two races easily, to finish his racing career at the age of five with a record of having won 19 of his 23 races, and collected about £30,000, beating some of the best horses in Europe. He was an unlucky third in the Prix de l'Arc de Triomphe of 1929, behind the Italian horse Ortello, and in the same year he equalled the record of the great Hungarian mare Kincsem by winning the Grosser Preis von Baden for the third year running. His son Pink Flower sired Wilwyn, who won 20 races and was the first horse to win the Washington D.C. International in America.

Oleander's influence continued well into the 1930's and 40's during the years when racing was not the most important thing taking place in Germany. His daughter Schwarzliesel won the German 1,000 Guineas and produced Schwarzgold, who won the German Derby by ten lengths, and his best representative in 1936 was Nereide, unbeaten in all her nine races, who defeated the colts in the German Derby as well as winning the 1,000 Guineas, the Oaks, and the Brown Ribbon, a race which from that year until 1944 was commemorated annually by the issue of a special postage stamp depicting the horse in some form.

In 1945, as the war was ending, racing came to a halt. It was resumed the next year but the German economy was at its lowest ebb, and the remarkable recovery that the finances of the country made as a whole did not for a long time extend to racing. Indeed, by 1953 there were serious fears about the future of the racing industry, and it was not until 1956 that those responsible for its future felt that the turning point might have been reached. The Federal Government at last began to show interest in racing and granted subsidies and concessions which allowed a 15 per cent increase in prize money. The average prize money per race crept up steadily from 3,110 DM in 1949 to 4,510 DM in 1961, and in that year Germany announced the Grosser Preis von Europa to be run in 1963 at Cologne, worth now 400,000 DM, in an attempt to get back into the international field.

From the announcement of the Preis von Europa, other countries seem to have become more aware of the prizes to be won in Germany, and in 1962 there was a minor invasion of the Iffezheim course at Baden-Baden, centre-piece of German racing in late August. Out of it came a victory for the English-trained Victorina in the Goldene Peitsche, a six furlongs sprint. It was the first time for 50 years that an English trained horse had appeared at Baden-Baden.

The following year Mr Gerry Oldham sent his five-year-old Espresso, trained by ex-jockey Harry Wragg, to win the Grosser Preis von Baden in a tight finish with Whippoorvill from France and Imperial, the massive Hungarian colt who is probably one of the best horses to come out of Central Europe since before the First World War.

The first running of the Preis von Europa went to a German horse, Opponent, but the successes of Victorina and Espresso had drawn attention to German racing and in 1965 the best horse that Russia has produced in recent years, Anilin, won the Preis von Europa, and a French horse Demi Deuil won the big prize at Baden-Baden. Anilin won the Preis von Europa race for three years running, while Gerry Oldham returned to Baden-Baden to win with Atilla and Salvo in 1966 and 1967.

Even though these international events must be good in the long run for German racing and breeding, giving the industry a yardstick against which to measure its progress, and an attraction for the public in the form of famous riders and horses from abroad, not all is well. Total prize money in 1968 had only just reached 11,000,000 DM, compared with the 11,400,000 DM of 1913, when money was worth a great deal more than it is now.

Germany itself has made several attempts to win international prizes since the Second World War. Countess Batthyany, whose horses were trained at Dortmund by Albert Klimscha, senior, rider of ten European Derby winners, sent her German Derby and Oslo Cup winner Orsini to Ascot in 1959 and saw him run fifth to Alcide in the King George VI and Queen Elizabeth Stakes, and there have been several German runners in the Washington D.C. International.

The year 1970 was an outstanding one for German horses abroad. Hitchcock, who finished fourth in the 1969 Washington D.C. International, remained in America to collect over $150,000 in distance races in New York and on the West Coast, while Priamos established himself as the best miler in Europe with victories in the Prix Dollar and the Prix Jacques le Marois, and the German filly won the Grand Prix de Deauville. The success of the German-bred Hibernia in the 1963 Irish Oaks was another indication that Germany was becoming an increasing influence in international racing.

Countess Batthyany, who won the Epsom Oaks in 1967 with Pia, moved some of her horses in training in 1965 from Germany to new quarters on the outskirts of Chantilly, understandably drawn by the honeypot of French racing, with its sound financial basis and big stakes.

Germany, like England, has not firmly grasped the nettle of the bookmaking problem. When we visited Cologne, there were no official bookmakers on the course, though unofficially it was understood that if you knew your way around, you could get a bet on with a bookie. Nearly half the tote betting was in forecasts. Off-course betting is legal in Germany, and there are some 140 licensed bookmakers, contributing a trifling amount in a form of betting levy to the sport on which they rely for their business.

Like the English bookmakers who descend on Longchamp on big race days and in spite of warnings from the French authorities carry on substantial business with their clients from home over for the day, German bookmakers make good money out of French racing. At one stage they

Lombard, one of many good horses produced by Germany's Gestut Schlenderhan. With the winner of the valuable Preis von Europa is his regular rider Fritz Drechsler.

had their own wireless station in Paris relaying French results to their betting shops.

There is little doubt that Germany has the ability to produce good horses, and has done so in the past. Bella Paola II, brilliant winner of the English 1,000 Guineas and Oaks, was largely of German breeding–her direct male line for the past four generations consisted of four German Derby winners–even though she was foaled in France and was trained there by Francois Mathet for the late M. Francois Dupre. When Germany solves the financial problems of its racing industry by obtaining a proper return from its betting turnover, it could regain the place that it held in world racing before the First World War.

Germany has pleasant racecourses, with a hedge replacing the usual inside rail, and many trees in the paddock area. Behind the stands a brass band often pumps out music between races, helping backers to forget their losers and soothing their brows as they peer for inspiration at their race-cards and morning papers. At some of the what are known as the "Ruhr-coal courses"–Dortmund, Dusseldorf, Gelsenkirchen-Horst, Cologne, Krefeld, Mulheim and Neuss,–one is conscious of a background of industry, with tall chimneys, pitheads and water cooling towers in the distance. The soil in the area between Dusseldorf and Cologne is also excellent and brood mares and foals graze in sheltered paddocks with an occasional glimpse of industrial activity through the trees.

The German Derby is run at Hamburg, now that Hoppegarten, which once held such an important place in German racing, is behind the Iron Curtain. Baden-Baden is German racing's biggest international occasion, though the Preis von Europa at Cologne brings a number of foreign visitors, human and equine. At Baden-Baden, Russian, German, French, Italian, Belgian, Spanish, English and Scandinavian horses compete, as well as those from behind the Iron Curtain, and the annual yearling sales are held. Germany has the foundation on which to build an important place in international racing. She will do that again when the matter of a proper return from the betting turnover to the industry is solved.

Italy's Contributions: Ribot and San Siro

They call San Siro, the racecourse on the outskirts of Milan, "the racecourse of truth". Probably Italy's two most important contributions to racing have been a championship racecourse which tests every ability of the horse, and a champion who won twelve races over it–Ribot.

Dead flat and with wide sweeping turns, San Siro has a run in of three and a half furlongs, slightly uphill, from the turn into the straight. Your horse must have the ability to gallop round bends as fair as any to be found in the world, and the stamina to face what may be a long drawn out battle to the winning post in front of the stone and marble grandstands.

Ribot, who features in the chapter on "Great Horses" later in this book, ground the opposition into that straight a dozen times and knew what it was like to stand in the San Siro unsaddling enclosure surrounded by the volatile Milan racegoers, who are equally capable of welcoming a hero with fervour or shouting "ladro" (thief) at a jockey on a beaten favourite.

Here are run two of Italy's most important races for three-year-olds and upwards, the Gran Premio di Milano, over 1 m. 7 f. in June, and the Gran Premio del Jockey Club in October. In recent years, Italian racing has begun to welcome international competitors as well as participating in foreign events with its own horses. A number of good French and English horses make the journey to Milan for these races, and several of them have journeyed on afterwards to Rome to run in the Premio Roma in early November over 1 m. 6 f.

One such was Chicago, owned by Switzerland-based financier Mr Gerry Oldham, and flown out from Harry Wragg's stables in Newmarket, England, in 1968 to be ridden by Australian Ron Hutchinson to victory in first the Gran Premio at Milan and then the big race in Rome.

Milan racecourse on a Sunday may be in competition with the huge football stadium across the road. (The chemist who deals with the dope tests at the hippodromo, incidentally, checks the urine of the footballers for substances which might be calculated to improve their performance on the field.) Nearby, also, is a trotting track which is under the supervision of the same organisation that controls the financial aspects of Italian racing, U.N.I.R.E., and does not, therefore, operate in competition.

Surrounded at the rear by trees, the San Siro grandstands are ornate. There is plenty of encouragement for the whole family to go racing, for the racecourse supplies a nursery, with pony and donkey rides, llamas pulling carts, swings and roundabouts. Admission is cheap.

For fathers and mothers with more serious problems, there are two ways of losing your money—with bookmakers (who are banned off course) and with the tote. The betting area is behind the stands. On the outside of the arena are the tote windows, and in the centre the bookmakers stand in what look like fairground booths with wooden canopies. In each stall there are three boards—one for win bets, one for place, and one for forecast betting, using a complex crisscross chart on which the probable odds against two selected horses finishing first and second are arrived at by following the line down from each of their numbers to a point at which they intersect.

There is little doubt that bookmakers the world over are identifiable. A bookie betting illegally at an Americans steeplechase meeting, in the heart of Virginia, looked as though he had stepped out of the East End of London. In fact, he came from Baltimore, and the prices he was offering would have got him lynched in Stepney. The one with whom we placed our bet at San Siro was a large man. He scribbled details of our bet on the ticket that he gave us. An undernourished clerk wrote the bet in his ledger and then gazed into the distance over the top of his spectacles while the boss went on shouting the odds.

By comparison with English bookmakers, the Italian layers do not make much noise, but there was a considerable din from the tote as tickets were punched out on machines looking like the beer pumps still to be found in English pubs. On the second race, we struck lucky and having collected our winnings from the tote, paid out in bank notes which looked large enough to pay off the mortgage on the house, we repaired to the bar.

Under no circumstances approach a racecourse barman on an Italian course and offer him money. You first have to negotiate with a cashier at the end of the bar. Tell her what you wish to drink, and she issues you with tickets to the value of beverages you intend to consume. These you pass to the barman, a resplendent gentleman in the uniform of a bandsman with the words Coca Cola embroidered discreetly on his breast-pocket. He accepts the tickets, pours your drink, and the trans-action is complete. The same rules apply whether you want a bottle of champagne or one of those small, deeply dark cups of coffee which can surprisingly quench your thirst in the hottest climates even better than a cold beer.

Close to San Siro there are many private training stables. After racing we visited those of Federico Regoli, one of five brothers who have ridden and trained in Italy. Federico rode for many years and was astride eight Italian Derby winners. He and other trainers at Milan work their horses on the well appointed training ground close to San Siro. Here there is an oval sand gallop, a steeplechase schooling ground, and a well watered oval turf gallop of nine furlongs, with a nine furlongs straight at one side. Mondays and Thursdays are the days allotted to work on the turf, and just before the gallops open at 8 a.m. several strings are circling round, waiting to go into action. A bell rings and the turf gallop immediately becomes a scene of great activity.

Besides staging the important races for older horses, Milan is responsible for three of Italy's six classic races—the Oaks d'Italia in early May, the Gran Premio d'Italia in early June, and the St Leger Italiano in late September. The Oaks and the St. Leger have recently been opened to foreign-bred horses.

The remaining three classics, the Premio Regina Elena and Premio Paroli, both over a mile in April and equivalent to the English One Thousand and Two Thousand Guineas, and the Derby Italiano, are staged at Rome's Cappanelle racecourse.

Here, against the background of the Castelli Hills, the best Italian three-year-olds are tested on a track, which if not quite as demanding as San Siro, still requires a horse which stays every inch of the journey.

The Derby Italiano is restricted to horses which were bred in Italy, but a gradual change is coming about in the Italian Jockey Club's policy over this matter of restriction, which has never proved sound wherever it has been applied. The elimination of competition from horses of other states or countries means that locally-bred horses are competing in a vacuum, with no yard-stick to measure them against the best that other countries can produce. Already the Italian Jockey Club has opened the Oaks and the St. Leger to foreign-bred horses, and it is to be hoped that they extend this soon to the other classic races. It can result only in a strengthening of the Italian racehorse, not a weakening.

Rome and Milan constitutes the major racing circuit in Italy, though there is racing too at Turin in the north, at Agnano on the outskirts of Naples, and on many minor tracks, while Merano caters exclusively for steeplechasers. Italy's most valuable steeplechase, the Grande Steeplechase di Milano, is however run on a typical sharp continental, figure of eight course in the centre of the San Siro track. A small stone wall and two jumps with fixed rails are among the obstacles, but most of the fences are undemanding of the horse.

A village which plays host every winter to the best horses in Italy, and sometimes from other countries, is that of Barbaricina, within a few miles of the famous leaning tower at Pisa. With fog, frost and snow visiting Milan, a 120 miles to the north and behind the Appennines all the leading trainers move their horses down to the milder climate of the Pisa area, at the mouth of the River Arno.

The village of Barbaricina has many stable yards in which in mid-February you can encounter an Italian Derby winner or one of the best two-year-olds of the previous season. The day on which we toured the winter quarters of the famous Razza Dormello-Olgiata and the Razza del Soldo, the rain fell from the skies, but it was mild and a complete contrast to the cold, foggy Milan that we had left by train a few hours earlier.

Barbaricina and the nearby Pisa racecourse have strong English connections. Thomas Rook, from Newmarket, went to Italy in 1896, to train for King Victor Emmanuel II, and laid out gallops and the racecourse in the grounds of the royal chateau at Barbaricina. He brought with him a number of English stable lads and their families, and today in Barbaricina names such as Smith, Wright and Murray are common in the village, though some of the families have gone out of racing.

Rook was not responsible for what is probably Pisa's greatest asset, a huge sandbank, some 150 ft. deep, which transformed the local landscape after the River Arno flooded some 2,000 years ago and centuries later provided a winter playground for Italy's thoroughbreds. The Pisa racecourse stands on this sand bank, and the going is virtually good all the time. A strong, tufted grass grows on it, and within a few hours of the heaviest rain, the water has drained through and the going returns to normal. Rook also had the forethought to put in a pipeline in 1900, which has recently been coupled to modern pumping equipment, and an unlimited supply of water allows the racecourse authorities to have some 40 sprinklers working on the course eight hours a day between April and October.

It was to Pisa that Irish trainer Vincent O'Brien sent both Pieces of Eight, winner of the Champion Stakes at Newmarket, and Sir Ivor, winner of the Epsom Derby and the Washington D.C. International, to winter, and they are among the many good horses which have worked up the famous "Straights", the ten furlongs gallops of both sand and turf, in the grounds of the old and now demolished palace. The quality of the horses which compete at Pisa during January and February is not always high, but the horses which lodge in the nearby village have been among the best in Europe.

Italian racing went through a difficult phase in the mid 1960's, with an admission tax forcing down attendances at racecourses and industrialists who maintained the biggest stables cutting down on their racing commitments. Then the Government removed the admission tax, and a bold step by the racing authorities in emptying their coffers to increase the prize money substantially revitalised the industry. There was a 14.86 per cent increase in stakes in 1969 over the previous year, and the result was that Italy became one of the most attractive places in the world to keep a horse in training from the financial aspect. At that stage, for every horse in training in Italy there was £1,200 in prize money to be won, compared with £550 in France, and £150 in England. The Italians have never been afraid to send their best horses, such as Ribot, Molvedo, Nearco and Tenerani, to France and England to race, and they hope to take steps to raise the status of their own racing by encouraging foreign horses to race on Italian tracks. Much depends on the efforts of the racing authorities to convince the Italian fiscal authorities that they should make a further reduction in the penal betting tax imposed in 1970 and which had a serious effect on betting turnover.

Russian Racing, for Points

On a summer Sunday afternoon the Muscovite goes out to seek recreation. While the streets of the Kremlin and the wide cobbled spaces of Red Square are filled with tourists from all parts of Russia, the Moscow dweller himself crowds the river steamers, swims in the open air pools or scooters out to his *dacha* in the country, returning in the twilight with a bunch of lilac dangling from the handlebars.

Many are drawn to the imposing Moscow Hippodrome, with its skyline of statues of rearing horses and line of fluttering flags, which promises a long afternoon of varied entertainment, with a card perhaps of twelve, or even sixteen events, divided between trotting and galloping.

The stand is modern, and was built in 1957. It has a massive, pillared portico and a rich and unfashionable solidity with elaborate decoration which fits the Moscow scene. It affords a perfect view of all parts of the course and entrance to the stand costs less than a rouble (40 p.).

The crowd spreads out over the restaurants and little snack bars, drinking sweet Russian champagne, and there is always a crush round the ice cream kiosks. The considerable crowd is out to enjoy itself, in the slow, sober way, with the flashes of quick humour and great patience to the children, which characterises a Russian crowd. Punters, like punters everywhere, give themselves over to concentrated study of the race-card.

The racecourse is right-handed and the circuit is six furlongs. The centre of the course, in which there are no obstructions for the viewer, is used for showjumping and other sports, which will probably be in progress at the same time as racing. The running rails have been replaced, as is usual in Europe, by low hedges.

The fine lawns of Ascot could not survive the Russian winters, and the grass of the parade ring is formed of coarse, quick-growing tufts. The few flowers, both planted and in pots, are the inevitable favourites of hard-winter countries such as quick-growing geraniums.

There are, of course, no owners in the Soviet Union as all the horses are the property of the State, and in many cases the jockey is also the trainer, so the jockeys stand around by themselves, while hero-worshipping small boys hover as near as they dare. The jockeys are tall and muscular, and the silks they wear, cut on the standard patterns, represent the studs at which the horses were bred, and are in simple combinations of colour. The horses themselves are rangy, powerful types, in noticeably hard condition.

You may bet, but on the tote, which is manned by brisk Russian women, who work out the winning odds at lightning speed on their clicking abacus. (We were surprised to find you can even buy lottery tickets in Communist Russia, sold by old women sitting at tables in the long, echoing underpasses below the main streets.) But betting is in miniscule quantities, in single units of one rouble. It is possible to bet for a win, or in doubles on the winners of consecutive races. There are no tipping newspapers, and the only guides to form are in the timings given for each horse in the racecard, and in the heads of the often very knowledgeable racegoers.

Horseracing was resumed in Russia in 1924 after the Revolution. Its object is to test the qualities of the horse in order to select the best stallions for breeding, to provide a yardstick by which the achievements of the various stud farms can be measured, and to provide "cultural relaxation" for the racegoer.

There are approximately 170 thoroughbred stallions and about 800 thoroughbred mares in the Soviet Union, while the number of thoroughbred horses in training is about 500.

There are 15 State stud farms, and the most valuable brood mares and the best stallions are concentrated at the crack Voskhod Stud Farm. The lines of Gainsborough, Blandford, Dark Ronald, Sunstar are among those represented, while the native lines of Tagor and Brimstone, which are noted for their solid build and staying qualities are established.

During the winter the horses are trained in groups of 25–30 on the stud farms. Each group has a trainer or trainer-jockey in charge, a second jockey and the necessary stable lads.

The best jockey to come out of the Soviet Union recently has been Georgian Nikolai Nasibov, who is well known abroad, having ridden in the Washington D.C. International and at Longchamp and Baden-Baden. He is now retired and is a trainer. Jockeys do a rigorous training. For three years they work as stable lads in summer and do theoretical work in winter. Then, if approved, may become apprentice jockeys, who ride in races both against each other and against fully-fledged jockeys. An apprentice has an allowance of about 8 lbs, and loses it only when he has ridden 300 winners (which usually takes about five years) or rides the winners of five of the 16 races which count as classics.

Racing takes place during the spring, summer and autumn, and the whole group, horses, jockeys, trainers and grooms, move as one unit to the racecourse, where they remain throughout the season.

The racecourses throughout the Soviet Union are graded as Union, Republic, Provincial, District and Local, and the importance of the races run there varies accordingly. The most important course is the Central Moscow racecourse, at which the All-Union prizes are run, and there are important courses at Pyatigorsk, Rostov and Lvov. Nearly all are dirt tracks, but there is a fine grass track at Lvov.

Some racecourses are kept for trotting, some for galloping, and some are combined. There are separate races for thoroughbreds, and for Arabs, Ter, Akhal-Tekin, Budenni, Don, Kabardin and other native breeds.

There are steeplechase tracks at Moscow, Tbilisi, Alma-Ata and a few other courses, and it will be remembered that the Russian steeplechasers Grifel and Reljef competed in the Grand National of 1961. It was not a successful venture as they had to carry top weight, not having qualified for handicapping by running in three races before publication of the weights.

In Russia competition between the studs is for points, which are awarded according to the importance of the races, and divided between first and second. Each point has a varying cash value of about 2 p at Moscow racecourse of which the winning jockey receives about 25% and the rest is divided between the stud and the stable lads. So there is a cash inducement, albeit not a large one, in addition to the natural rivalry between the studs.

All the races are condition or weight for age races, and there are no handicaps. Two-year-old colts carry 57 kg (9st. or 126 lb.), three-years-olds 58 kg (9st. 2 lb. or 128 lb.) and older horses 59 kg (9st. 4 lb. or 130 lb.). Fillies carry 2 kg (4½ lb.) less.

Races are made up of horses of the same age, grouped according to ability. On arrival at the racecourses, two-year-olds begin racing in the fourth group. After the first win, or after coming in second twice, the horse is transferred for subsequent races to the third group, and after the next win to the second group and so on. Horses which show outstanding form race outside groups, and are entered for the major and classic races.

The most coveted and valuable races are:–The Kalinin Memorial Race for two-year-olds, run over 1600 metres (1 mile) and identical with the Grand Criterium in many countries.
The Bolshoi Letnii (Great Summer) Prize for three-years-olds, run over 1600 metres (1 mile) and identical with the English 2,000 Guineas.
The Neva River Prize for three-year-old fillies over the same distance. (One Thousand Guineas.)
The Bolshoi Vasesoyuznyi (Great All Union) for three-year-olds run over 2,400 metres (1½ miles). This race, which has been run since 1924, is equivalent to the Derby. In pre-Revolution Russia

Portentous entrance to Moscow racecourse (above).
Anilin, the best racehorse bred in Russia. Winner three years running of the Preis von Europa at Cologne, he also ran second in the Washington D.C. International at Laurel, Maryland.

it was known as the Bolshoi Vserossiiski (Great All-Russia), and has been run in Moscow since 1886.
The Volga River Prize for three-year-old fillies over 2,400 metres (1½ miles). (The Oaks.)
The Marshall of the Soviet Union S.M. Budenni Prize for three-year-olds over 2,800 metres (1¾ miles). (The St. Leger.)
The Elita Prize for four-year-olds and upwards over 2,400 metres (1½ miles).
The U.S.S.R. Prize over 3,200 metres (2 miles).

Russian horses have long dominated racing in Eastern Europe, winning the giant's share of the Easter European championship meeting, which moves from capital to capital–Moscow, Warsaw, Prague, Berlin and Budapeste. In 1958 they turned their attention also to the west, and the success of their horses, and in particular of Anilin, has aroused interest there in Russian thoroughbreds and Russian racing. This tough, whiteblazed brown horse by Element out of Analogichnaya, has travelled and raced widely abroad. In 1965 he won the Preis von Europa at Cologne and, as a five-year-old, in 1966 he repeated this success, just beating the good English horse Salvo, trained by Harry Wragg, to whom he was conceding five pounds more than weight for age. He then finished second in the Laurel International at Washington D.C., where, after leading throughout, he was overhauled by the French Behistoun. Anilin again won at Cologne in 1967.

It was, however, Zabeg (by Baltic Baron, grand-son of the Hungarian-bred Blanc), third in the Laurel International in 1960, who was the first Russian horse of recent times to make an impact abroad. He has been accepted by the American stud book, and now stands in the United States.

The importance of exporting thoroughbreds and also native Russian horses as a means of earning foreign currency is increasingly recognised in Russia, where sales for foreign buyers are held in Moscow each September. Buying at these sales is possible only in foreign currency. Each prospective purchaser is provided with a numbered wooden board, which he must raise to make a bid and which identifies him should he be the successful bidder.

Like Japan, Russia is not afraid to send its best horses to run on foreign racecourses in an attempt to make a mark in the world of international racing, and it is also keen to sell its thoroughbred stock to other countries. Horses such as Anilin and Zabeg have shown that Russia can produce animals which can hold their own at least against the best in Eastern Europe, at Cologne, and make a respectable showing in America. They will probably improve.

The Tradition of Hungarian Racing

It was Baron Henri de Gelsey who convinced us that Hungarian racing in the late 19th century was nearly the best in the world. The Baron, expatriated, stout and fussy, lived in a book-lined flat in London, wrote excellent articles for the British Racehorse, loved talking about the Hungary that he remembered, and then died in 1966, after presenting us with the set of stamps commemorating the great Hungarian mare Kincsem and a back number of the American Racing Manual. Slowly the image of Hungarian racing began to fade without the Baron there to remind us of its greatness. It was all probably the nostalgic dreamings of an old man. And then, into London in 1968 came Mr Tibor Brody from Budapest, bearing photographs of Hungarian racing, and testifying that the Baron was right.

We have yet to visit Rakosi racecourse, almost in the heart of Budapest, or Alag, the training centre some 15 miles away. But this chapter is being included as a tribute to a country that undoubtedly held a high place in European racing in its formative years–and produced Kincsem, who features in the section on Great Racehorses.

Mr Brody affirmed that the great period of Hungarian racing was between 1870 and 1890. It then stood about third in importance in Europe, behind England and France, until German racing improved its standard during the last decade of the 19th century and in the years before the First World War. Standing outside the main game, his ratings for the European league at the moment are: France, England, Germany, Italy, Russia and Hungary.

Hungary at the time that he visited London was bouyant about the performances of the massive Imperial, who had almost snatched the Grosser Preis von Baden from Espresso and whose sire Imi, a superbly handsome horse was beaten only once. Imi's sire, Intermezzo, was found pulling a peasant's cart after the Second World War at a time when the injection of 25 thoroughbreds, recovered from Germany by the Americans, was a welcome addition to the sadly depleted Hungarian racehorse population.

Bookmakers were declared illegal in Hungary in 1958 and with a steadily improving financial position, the thoroughbred population has grown from only 54 in 1946 to 450 broodmares alone today. In 1968, for the first time for many years, Hungary had representatives at Newmarket buying brood mares in foal.

Rakosi racecourse is one of the best in Europe– a flat galloping circuit, with wide turns and a four furlongs run in to the winning post. The Hungarian classics are run on an English pattern with colts and fillies races over a mile in the Spring, the Derby over 1½ miles on the third Sunday in June, and a St. Leger over 1m. 6f. in September.

Mr Edwin Hesp, chief secretary of the "Direktorium" that controls Hungarian racing in place of the Jockey Club, disbanded under Russian influence after the war, is a grand-son of Englishman Robert Hesp, who trained the great Kincsem, and there are many descendants in Hungarian racing of the Englishmen who were training or working there when it was in its full glory–the Hitchcocks, the Adams, the Reeves and the Bensons.

The Scandinavian Circuit

Racing in Scandinavia forms a fairly close circuit, with the best horses and jockeys of Norway, Sweden and Denmark regularly visiting the courses of each country. Jealously guarding the limits of each racing season is the Scandinavian winter, which seldom permits the start of racing before the middle of May in Sweden and Norway, or before mid April in Denmark. Dates in Norway, for instance, are flexible, and racing starts in the Spring when the course at Ovrevoll near Oslo is clear of snow, and goes on into November so long as the snow does not return.

There are strong links between racing in the British Isles and that in Scandinavia. At every sale of horses in training and breeding stock at Newmarket you can see mammoth articulated horse boxes bearing number plates from Oslo, Copenhagen and Stockholm, waiting to take purchases back via the North Sea ferries. English-bred stallions were responsible for the winners of no fewer than 17 of the 21 Scandinavian classic races run between 1962 and 1968. An exceptional year was 1966, when the Danish Derby went to Eminent, by the French sire Souverain; the Norwegian Derby to Neckman, by Nektar of German descent; while the Swedish race went to Svenor. by Stratos, bred by the Norwegian ship owner Mr J.J. Lorentzen at his stud in the south of Sweden.

Far Bell, winner of the 1967 Danish Derby, too, was by a Scandinavian-bed horse called Far West who won all three Scandinavian Derbys in 1950, but generally the tough climate is not helpful to breeding and there has to be constant replenishment of stock.

Sweden took steps in 1963 to defeat the long winter and lengthen their racing season. They prepared a straw covering to the dirt track at Taby, just outside Stockholm with its smart American style grand stand opened in 1960. The snow covered straw, rolled and tended, affords a surprisingly good surface giving an opportunity for enthusiastic racegoers to continue their enjoyment of the sport, and moderate horses which were not able to win during the main part of the season to pick up some prize money and pay their fodder bills. Even if the horses are moderate, they present a handsome spectacle against a snowy background.

The summers of Scandinavia are warm and

enjoyed to the full, but for winter sport at Taby, racegoers have to wrap well against the cold, with woollen stockings drawn over nylons, fur and interlined coats, and hats and caps ingeniously incorporating ear-muffs. The air is like champagne, but racegoers welcome the braziers which melt circles of snow in the enclosures as they stand trying to decide on their selections for the next race.

Scandinavian jockeys tend to be lanky and bigboned. Riders from England are much in demand for big races on Sundays, the day on which most of the big events take place. Bent Hansen caused a minor sensation when he rode the Danish-trained Wonderboy in the Washington D.C. International in America in 1961. When Bent raised his arm to shoulder height, champion American rider Johnny Longden could stand upright beneath it, with room to spare.

At a week-end, if you stand in the European departure building at London Airport, you will see half of English racing passing through, bound for the big races of France, Germany and Scandinavia. Eight English and Australian jockeys rode in a special race at Stockholm to commemorate the British Trade Fair in 1962, and since then there has been a steady flow of overseas riders to Scandinavian courses. Probably a record was set at Norway's Ovrevoll courses in 1970 when on one Sunday 17 English jockeys, more than half of them visitors for the day, the others based in Scandinavia, rode in various races.

Norwegian racing has made considerable strides in recent years under the guidance of the ambitious President of the Jockey Club, Mr Einar Tidemand-Johannessen, and with tote turnover and attendances showing a substantial increase (bookmaking is not permitted) the sport there is in a more buoyant state than in neighbouring countries. The launching of the Norwegian Grand National in 1970 was a great success, resulting in four runners being flown over from England and one contestant arriving from Germany (the race went to the Swedish horse Sorrento, ridden by English jockey David Nicholson). While some of the more conservative members of the Jockey Club expressed doubts about the trend when Happy Hunter became the first English horse to defeat the local horses in the Derby and the St. Leger that year, there is little doubt that this trend towards international competition can, in the long run, be only of benefit to Norwegian and Scandinavian racing.

The late King of Sweden studying his racecard and discussing form at Tagersrö racecourse, near Malmo, on Derby Day.

The start at Hamburg, Derby Day, 1971. Many countries are replacing "barrier" starts with starts from stalls, which are safer for jockey and horse, ensure that the runners are all pointing in the same direction, and give that valued customer, the punter, a better run for his money than the old type of start.

Winter races on the frozen lake
at St. Moritz, Switzerland

The Jockeys' World

For all the planning that goes into a race by breeder, owner, trainer, for all the prognostications of the press and prayers of the punter, there is one man who holds in his two hands the final answer to what can happen out there on the track, and that is the jockey.

Once the trainer gives him a leg up into the saddle in the paddock, a last word of instruction before watching him ride out through the gate onto the course, the jockey is the one who controls the destiny of hundreds of thousands of bets, the dreams and fortunes of the man who bred the horse and the man who owns him, the reputation of the man who has spent hours in planning its training and its placing in a series of races which can enhance or debase its value.

For the jockey it may be just another race—a bad horse racing against other bad horses. Or it may be the ride he has been thinking and dreaming about for the last month—planning every move in the race, where to be at the first bend, when to move up to the leaders, when to take the lead, worrying all the time whether he can overcome the horse's tendency to hang to the right in a driving finish.

And it is all happening at perhaps 35 miles an hour, with other horses using to their utmost all their 1200lb of muscle and bone on either side, sometimes a biting wind penetrating the jockey's silk jacket or numbing his fingers gripping the reins. Decisions to be made in a fraction of a second which may decide whether a jockey wins the race, finishes in the stewards room, or on a stretcher.

Jockeys today are a sophisticated crowd compared to the midgets of 350 years ago who were put up on some of the giants of the past to pilot them in match races over four miles. Fed on gin in their youth to keep them small, some of them weighed only 42lb., and it is incredible that they managed to stay on their powerful mounts, let alone to steer them round corners.

Not all the old time jockeys were midgets, but weight, or lack of it, has always been a factor in the life of the jockey. Continual wasting and deptivation depressed Fred Archer, champion English jockey from 1874 to 1886, so much that he committed suicide. Today, many top jockeys live a life of purgatory compared to the well-fed owners whose horses they ride, eating as their main meal something that most people would regard as an adequate hors d'oeuvre, and spending hours in a sweatbox.

Jockeys in paintings and photographs up to the last years of the 19th century look quaint, sitting upright, their legs full length into stirrups which came below the horse's rib cage, their bodies offering the maximum wind resistance as they urged their mounts along.

It was coloured boys at American country race meetings who developed the short-legged style of the modern jockey. Thrown up onto the backs of saddleless, bridleless horses, they naturally leant forward to clutch the horse's mane and gripped the withers with their knees. Crouched thus, they achieved several things inherent in the modern jockey's style—streamlining, a powerful grip at the knees, and positioning of the bulk of their weight over a point better constructed to carry it than the middle of the horse's back.

English jockeys continued to ride in the old manner until the arrival on the scene from America in 1897 of Tod Sloan, who rode some 20 winners in a short period in the autumn of that year and returned the next year to ride for Lord William Beresford. He was never champion jockey in the short while that he was permitted to ride in England (the Stewards disapproved of, among other things, his betting habits), but his success convinced English jockeys of the advantages of his style.

Today the first thing that a young rider wants to do when he joins a training stable is to pull up his stirrup leathers until his knees are tucked under his chin so that he resembles a Lester Piggott, a Willie Shoemaker or a George Moore. Knowing trainers discourage this tendency in the early days, trying rather to encourage basic principals of horsemanship, but if a lad is any good it will not be long before he is riding out in the mornings to exercise, whistling between his teeth, knees up, and looking down the neck of a nodding thoroughbred who cost a lot more to bring into the world than he did himself.

Small stature, small bones, and small parents—these are three basic qualifications that the hopeful young jockey needs. The indications that he will not grow too large to follow his trade, but also a natural affinity with horses, and a sense of dedication. Success has come easily to some jockeys, but not to many.

For the thousands whose love of horses and small stature lures them into the racing game as stable lads and hotwalkers, perhaps a tenth ever ride a horse in a race and a tenth of that band ever ride a winner. For those who make the grade, the rewards can be enormous.

In 1953, America's leading jockey, Willie Shoemaker, rode in 1,683 races, and won 485 of them. Ten per cent of the prize money won by his mounts that year earned him $178,418.

For most who get to the top, the early years

The inelegant, upright, wind-resistant style favoured by jockeys until the end of the 19th century (above).
The crouched and streamlined style, introduced to England from America by Tod Sloan in the 1890s.

Fred Archer, champion English jockey from 1874 to 1886, committed suicide in a fit of depression caused by constant wasting (above).
Australian riders have had a big influence on British racing. These are seven who were riding in England in 1965—Bill Williamson, Jack Purtell, Garnie Bougoure, Scobie Breasley, Bill Pyers, Eddie Cracknell and Ron Hutchinson.

have been heart breaking at times. Sent from home to work in stables at an early age, riding out on frosty mornings with numbed fingers, mucking out, cleaning the yard, taking the trainer's wife's poodle for a walk, and trying to resist the temptation of eating a buttered roll along with the morning coffee.

A lad apprenticed to a leading Newmarket trainer often may not ride a racehorse for several months after joining the stable, even if he arrives with good horsemanship already instilled through childhood experience with ponies out hunting and in the show ring.

Observation of him riding one of the stable hacks or a pony will soon show the trainer or his head lad whether the boy is capable of sitting on a volatile racehorse, able to accelerate to 35 miles an hour in four huge leaps and with the wide open spaces of Newmarket Heath around him. Once a boy has learned how to ride out in a string of perhaps 30 other horses, to gallop one with a half a dozen others at the pace required by the trainer, and to balance him so that he can produce his best effort at the end of the gallop, then the trainer may think about giving the lad a ride in a race in public.

That first visit to the jockeys' room at a racecourse is a daunting experience for a young rider. He is unsure of the routine, does not know where to sit, where to hang his clothes, what to do with the saddle. But there are always the jockeys' valets, who travel from meeting to meeting looking after riders and their equipment, laundering breeches, polishing boots, mending and stitching and always arriving the next day in good time with everything in order. One of them will take the young apprentice under his wing and see that he arrives in the parade ring in good order.

The first ride can be an exhilarating experience, or a depressing one. To come under starter's orders with perhaps Gordon Richards on your left and Lester Piggott on your right and to find halfway up the straight that your horse is going equally as well as that ridden by one of these champions—then all those cold mornings and boring hours of drudgery begin to have a meaning.

To ride back to the unsaddling enclosure on a winner at this stage in a boy's career is enough to justify everything that has happened to date, to send him to the phone to give a graphic account to fond parents who have seen his name in print for the first time in the racing results in the evening paper, and to drive to desperation his less fortunate fellow stable lads who have to bear with his stories of how he beat the champions, until a good thump on the left ear brings him back to the realities of working in stables.

"Getting away with it" is an expression used

among struggling English jockeys for someone for whom everything falls into place at the right time, so that he is recognised by the professional racing element important to him—the owners, trainers and press—and breaks through into the magic circle of those riders in demand.

The order in which things happen in a young jockey's life can have a terrifying affect on his destiny in a lucrative trade. One may ride three winners in quick succession for a well-known owner, then break a leg in a fall, and see the horses he has won on succeeding under another rider, making it necessary for him to start all over again when he returns to the saddle. Or success and headlines may lead to a crescendo of successes, so that within months of riding his first winner, the apprentice is a household name and is earning large sums of money.

Today's jockeys are men who travel enormous distances every year. Australian jockeys, in great demand in Europe for their inbuilt judgement of pace, have found top jobs in England, Ireland and France, and regularly commute between those countries, as well as Italy, Germany, Belgium and Scandinavia. Lester Piggott, eight times champion in England, rides in France sometimes on as many as four days in one week, but in one winter may also have winning rides in South Africa, South America, Singapore, Australia, and New Zealand.

The top American jockeys such as Willie Shoemaker cross and re-cross the continent, increasingly meeting in the jockeys' room on the major tracks riders from South America. In fact, a Spanish or Portuguese interpreter is now almost one of the essentials whenever a stewards' inquiry is held on an American track involving evidence from riders.

Wherever jockeys come from, whether they ride the "acey-ducey" style, with one stirrup leather longer than the other in countries where they always race on left-handed tracks, or if they need the vast variety of knowledge of tracks of different shapes and indulations as in Europe, they face much the same problems: – the dangers of a fall at high speed, for the most the need to keep to a frugal diet; and how to break into the big time. For those who make it, the privations are usually daunting, the rewards rich.

The greatest of them all. Sir Gordon Richards, who rode 4,870 winners, on Pinza, his Epsom Derby winner of 1953 (above).
Even champions hit the deck. Lester Piggott descends from Barbary Pirate at Brighton, England, after the saddle had slipped near the winning post.

Willie Shoemaker, who has ridden more winners than any jockey in history, arrives for the day's work at the jockey's quarters, Hollywood Park, Los Angeles. (right) Cool, tough, calculating Lester Piggott, nine times English champion jockey, rides freelance, studies the form book hard and travels wherever he sees a winning chance.

Clerks of the scales at Newmarket (above) and Longchamp (below) check returning jockeys

Face of "The Shoe", Willie Shoemaker

Between races, jockeys relax at Tokyo racecourse (top). Young jockeys go out for their first rides in public at Newmarket; and (right) a tense group, Yves St.-Martin, trainer Francois Mathet and owner the Aga Khan, wait in the parade ring at Longchamp.

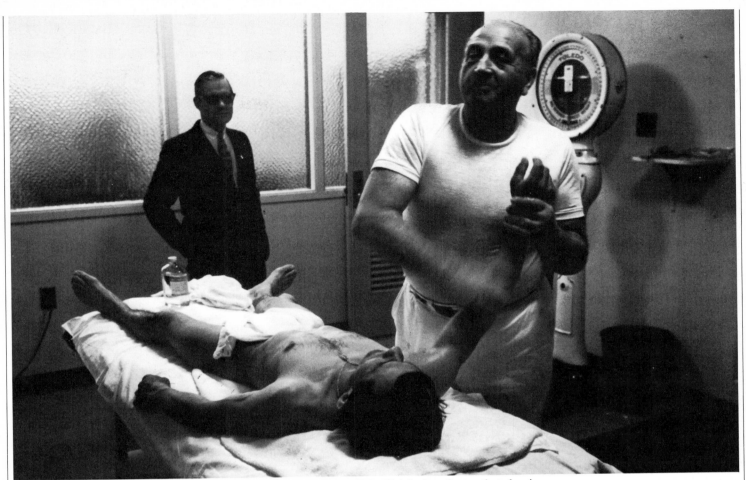

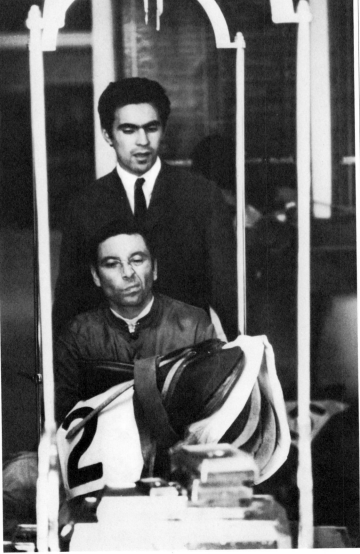

Weight is a factor that dominates the life of the jockey. Dieting and sweating is part of the daily round. Hollywood Park, Los Angeles, provides a sauna bath to help jockeys with weight problems, and a masseur as well. Below, a jockey climbs on the scales at Palermo racecourse, Buenos Aires.

Waiting to go out at Hollywood Park (left). Top jockeys on American courses are "confined to barracks" once they arrive before racing and cannot mix with the public. Cards, pool, chess, help to pass the time before and between races. Lower picture shows guard who is in charge of the saddle and weights from the time the jockey weighs out until the moment of saddling.

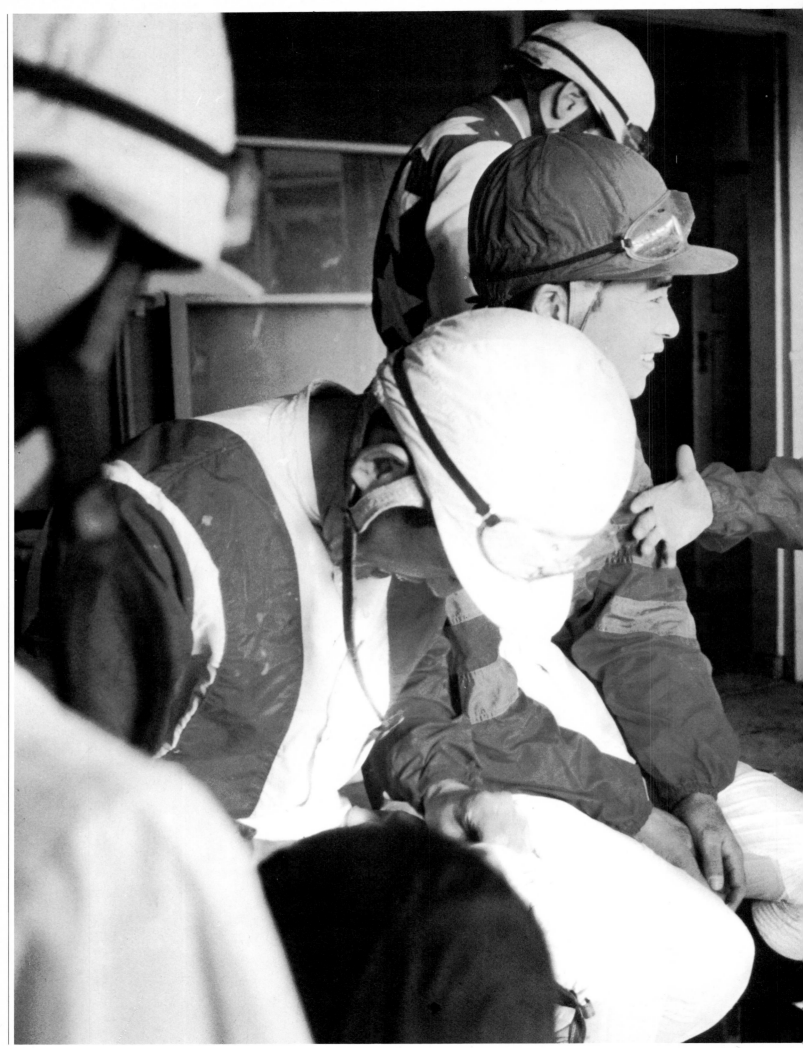

"So I said to this jockey, move over please, and he did, and I won"

Driving finish, American style

American Racing— a Multi-Million Dollar Business

When you talk about American racing, you move into the realm of huge numbers: the paid attendance at American race tracks in 1969 was over 45 million; the public wagered nearly four billion dollars with the pari mutuels during the year; an estimated three billion dollars are invested in some 30,000 racehorses; racetracks pay some 370 million dollars to state governments in taxation; they have an annual payroll of more than 380,000,000 dollars. And so on. Figures which are staggering in any other racing country, with perhaps the exception of France, are commonplace in America. Big money reigns supreme and at first glance the horse himself takes second place.

There are 138 race tracks in America—almost twice as many as there were in 1954—spread out from Playfair and Longacres in the Northwest, Rockingham Park and Brockton Fair in the Northeast, down to Tropical Park, southernmost of the Florida tracks, and Del Mar, close to California's Mexico border. Yet racing is illegal in 22 American states, including Texas where the horse has played a bigger part in local history than in any other state. In spite of the attraction of the millions of dollars which can be made available to the legislatures for road building, hospitals and schools through the taxation of parimutuel betting, the "antis" and religious groups have so far managed to thwart the ambitions of the Texas Racing Association and similar groups in many other states which have sought for years to establish in their area the sport which on a nation-wide basis attracts more customers than any other rival spectator sport. For even without legalised parimutuel racing in so many states (you can stage races at a country or state fair but you must not bet on them) horse racing is way ahead of other sports on attendances. With 70 million spectators in 1969, it was 32 million ahead of its nearest rival, professional football.

American racing had its birth in the main street of Jamestown, Virginia, and later on the farm tracks of the narrow toehold that the English settlers established on the vast American continent early in the 17th century. At first, down the broad main street of Jamestown, Englishmen, seeking relaxation from their battles with the forest of Virginia and the native tribes, matched the few horses they had in quarter-mile dashes. But the spur-of-the-moment matches which suddenly developed as the result of arguments over the respective merits of horses, soon resulted in a statute banning racing in the street, and they were moved to farm tracks, often between fences only four or five yards apart. Any stretch of ground just over a quarter of a mile long was good enough and the horses needed rapid acceleration from a standing start and the ability to pull up quickly. These are still the attributes of the participants in quarter horse racing, the direct descendant of these early Virginian contests, which are today popular features at country fairs and many Western tracks in America.

But for the ancestry of modern American racing, you really have to move on some 50 years from these early quarter horse races at Jamestown, to 1665, the year after a British expeditionary force under Colonel Richard Nicolls, had ousted the Dutch from New York and had set about anglicising the area. The policy included changing Dutch place names to English, and so it was on a flat area called Salisbury Plain that the colony's first race meeting was held. This was still some 50 years before the Byerly Turk, the Darley Arabian and the Godolphin Barb stood at stud in England and established the line of the thoroughbred which was to spread out to every country in the world. So the horses that raced on Salisbury Plain were probably of somewhat common origin. But at least they had the best to gallop on, for a contemporary description of the two miles round race track says that it had an "elastic, tough, carpet-like covering, which the horse in his gallops does not cut through, yet offering sufficient foothold"—not unlike a description of the usually perfect going on the present, quiet country Salisbury racecourse in England.

Importations of bloodstock to America were slow—the shipping space was needed for human beings and their supplies—but the population of horses capable of both doing a day's work and going a fair gallop for the purposes of entertainment gradually increased. The English Jockey Club of more recent years has not, incidentally, been alone in giving horse racing a dignity beyond that of mere show business, because Colonel Nicolls, in decreeing that there should be race meetings in the New York area, is on record as saying that this was not only a diversion but also for "encouraging the bettering of the breed of horses". Since that day a vast industry has grown up on this wonderful pretence—that horse racing exists for the improvement of racehorses. But who cares—we only know that it is a highly entertaining way of improving anything.

The first thoroughbred to reach America did not arrive until 1730, and was Bulle Rock, a stallion who was imported to Virginia. But the first to have any serious effect on the breed was Fearnought, who arrived 99 years after Colonel Nicolls' inaugural race meeting at Salisbury Plain, which had by this time changed its name to Hempstead Plains.

By the beginning of the present century, there were many similarities between the American and English racing set-ups, though, even at this stage, American managements seem to have realised the visual attraction of racing, and that huge sprawling courses on which many of the races started in the next county were far less fun for the spectator than a compact circuit on which the runners are never more than half a mile away from the stands. The sport was ruled by the American Jockey Club. Bookmakers were part of the American racing scene, there were fearless bettors whose tilts against the odds-layers would match the best efforts of the great gamblers of English society.

American jockeys developed a streamlined, balanced style of riding which was at first greeted with derision when they appeared on English courses in the early part of the century, but as it got results, it eventually changed the style of English riders who had until then sat almost bolt upright and ridden with long stirrup leathers. There was recognition, too, that American racehorses might be a bit better than people back in England might have supposed. Sporting Life writer Edward Moorhouse begrudgingly conceded when he visited America in 1906, "I am willing to admit that the American horse is not the social pariah he is generally supposed to be."

Bookmakers began to disappear from American racetracks from the late 1930's and since then all the on-course betting has been through the pari–mutuels, operated by the racetracks themselves. This was the turning point in the finances of the sport but had to happen in a way which emphasises one essential difference between the ways in which English and American racing were, and are, governed. Each American state which permits parimutuel racing, has its own racing laws, and whereas the English Jockey Club governs racing completely, making the rules, licensing courses, participants and officials, the American Jockey Club has not been allowed to develop in the same way. It was formed in 1893 as racing's supervisory and rule-making body, but in 1930 a New York court decision robbed it of its power to license racing participants. Its rules now apply solely to racing in the states of New York and Delaware, and though they are the outline on which most racing rules are based, they have no power in other states. The Jockey Club's chief function now is in the registration of thoroughbreds and the maintenance of the American Stud Book, and each state requires registration papers from the Club before a horse is permitted to take part in a race.

Within each state, racing is governed by a Racing Commission responsible to the State Governor, and controlled in its actions by the legislature and the state courts. A National Association of State Racing Commissioners formed in 1934 provides a bureau for information on suspensions, fines and disqualifications within the industry, and its annual convention discusses racing rules which it is hoped will become uniform, but it also is faced with the problem that member states may be unwilling to accept these rules. It continually amazes those within and without American racing that the sport has, under the circumstances, developed into the biggest crowd-puller on the American continent and earned the respect of other countries for the way in which its racing is policed and controlled.

The growth in attendances, and thus the money available for all sections of the industry has been phenomenal in the last 25 years, and it has primarily been caused by recognition a long time ago that the most important person in American racing is the man who goes through the turnstiles. Give him a track at which he can park his car with ease, eat and drink in comfort, bet and watch the racing without going out in the rain, and where the horses are never more than three furlongs away from the end of his nose, and he is happy. We will never forget the look of amazement on the face of an American racing newspaper editor when we showed him the Cesarewitch course at Newmarket, England, where the horses start about a mile and three-quarters from the stand, disappear behind a big bank, and then re-appear to race straight towards the enclosures for more than nine furlongs. "How the hell do you get people to come and watch racing here?" he asked.

Fitting happily into the big money atmosphere of American racing is Aqueduct, the New York Racing Association's mammoth race track a couple of miles away from Kennedy Airport. While the big jets thunder in and out, up to 73,435 New York racing fans will bet something like 5½ million dollars on a card of nine races. Subway trains run from the centre of New York out to Aqueduct's special station where they disgorge the hordes of people, leaving the carriage floors crackling underfoot with a carpet of peanut shells. From an inter-airport helicopter, Aqueduct looks like a busy anthill. From the saddling paddock down by the track, the vast stand dominates everything, like an aircraft carrier standing at a wooden jetty.

Within the stand the parimutuel windows devour the queues and their money; down in the lower levels a money-counting machine chatters through the afternoon. Aqueduct's stewards are the most professional in the world. They watch over 2,000 races a year, know just what they are looking at on their camera patrol screen, admonish jockeys, instruct apprentices with re-runs of races in their well-appointed private cinema, and hand out judgements dispassionately.

Aqueduct is the home of more $100,000 races than any other track in the country, and was the temporary home of the classic Belmont Stakes, while Belmont Park was out of action for rebuilding in recent years. The annual betting turn-over is around 690 million dollars at Aqueduct, neighbouring Belmont Park and up-state Saratoga, and they hand over some 80 million dollars tax to New York State every year. The politicians regard racing as a money-making machine and the New York Racing Association is continually under pressure to stage even more racing than the 208 days recorded at Belmont and Aqueduct in 1969.

Aqueduct has been described as cold, impersonal, a racing supermarket, a betting machine, in contrast to neighbouring Belmont Park, tree-surrounded and carefully re-built to preserve its atmosphere. While we defy anyone to love the place, the fact remains that year in and year out hundreds of thousands of New Yorkers enjoy racing at Aqueduct. It is in character with the city that produced it.

At Aqueduct, and many other tracks these days, you can observe that strange phenomenen–the man who pays to enter a racetrack, and then watches most of the racing on a television set. Closed circuit television is a blessing at large tracks, where it is not always possible for patrons to see the horses in the parade ring, keep an eye on totalisator odds, and queue to place a bet in the interval between races. But we thought the height of absurdity had been reached when we saw a racegoer at Aqueduct watching a race through binoculars–not out on the track but on one of the closed circuit screens some distance away from him.

Public relations plays an important part in the operation of a racetrack, and the New York Racing Association maintains a busy publicity department. Racing has to fight hard to command space in daily newspapers in competition with other sports, and everything possible is done to see the pressmen covering the sport get all the information they need. The facilities in the press box at Aqueduct and Belmont Park include a television set which is a repeater of the picture the stewards are looking at when they hold an enquiry into the running of a race. The press thus see the same

Governor Nicolls established America's first race meeting at Hempstead Plains on Long Island "to encourage the bettering of the breed of horses"— which is as good a reason as any for holding a horse race (above).
Match races are seldom seen these days, but in the 19th century they were the spice of racing. This tryptiche depicts the famous match for 20,000 dollars between American Eclipse and Henry on Long Island in 1823. According to this print, on linen, Henry won two of the three four mile heats, but all the records show that in fact American Eclipse was the winner.

visual evidence that helps the stewards reach a decision in a case of bumping or crossing. "I must say that I was opposed to this at first" steward Francis P. Dunne told us "but in operation it has worked out well. The press now see the same evidence as ourselves and I believe it has increased confidence in us–and possibly increased our vigilance!"

For 24 days every summer, the play moves up-state to Saratoga Springs. This is a charming change of scenery. Saratoga is surrounded by shady trees, people become less professional, more relaxed. The natives also see the visitors coming and up the prices 300 per cent.

The Saratoga Yearling Sales occupy several evenings after racing, the big money buyers are there in force for what is increasingly an inter-national gathering, and those who can afford a bungalow, enjoy sitting out having drinks before racing or the sales, watching the world go by and gossiping about great horses, horse deals and the people who make up the racing world. Saratoga boasts the oldest stakes race in the United States, the Travers, which was instituted in 1864 and won by many good horses including Man o' War, the grey Native Dancer, and Buckpasser. There is an old-world look about the modernised Saratoga stands, for in the re-building care was taken not to spoil the atmosphere. Saratoga is also the home of the National Museum of Racing, enshrining many racing relics and thoroughbred paintings.

Down in New Jersey you can go racing at Atlantic City, a few miles from the ocean and a place where flowers and shrubs have been used to the greatest advantage. If you are going to lose your money you could not do it in prettier sur-roundings than at Atlantic City. The track was not built until 1946, but has established a reputation for good racing on turf in a country where the dirt track dominates. A look at the records shows that Mongo, winner of the Washington D.C. Inter-national at Laurel in 1963, prefaced that victory with a record 1 min. 48 seconds over 9 furlongs on the beautifully kept Atlantic City turf, and the $62\frac{3}{5}$ seconds clocked by Isaduchess in August 1965 still stands as a world record for $5\frac{1}{2}$ fur-longs on turf.

One of the best run and most profitable race-tracks on the Eastern seaboard is also in New Jersey. This is Garden State, close to Philadelphia, where three races alone, the Garden State Stakes for two-year-olds, the Gardenia for juvenile fillies and the Trenton for older horses are responsible for prize money totalling over 550,000 dollars. Like Atlantic City, Garden State is in a densely populated area, and every effort is made by the promotional side of the operation to secure the leisure dollars of the local inhabitants.

One of the best-known of American tracks throughout the world is Laurel, Maryland. Back in 1950 nobody outside America had heard of the place, and it was not going well. It was acquir-ed from the Maryland Jockey Club by Morris Schapiro, who emigrated from Hungary at the turn of the century, and who had hauled himself up in the true American tradition to become chairman of the Boston Metals Company of Baltimore and the National Metal and Steel Corporation of Los Angeles. His son John Schapiro became President of Laurel and through his efforts in 1952 was born the Washington D.C. International, one of many attempts to have been made before and since to establish an international horse contest in America.

The only difference about this race was that it worked, largely because of the hard work and belief in what he was doing of the man at the top, and partly because of the piece of luck that one of the foreign challengers, Wilwyn from Great Britain, won the first running of this expensive venture, and a French horse, Worden II, was successful the following year.

The prize money crept up, and by 1959 the foreigners were beginning to face real competition from the American-trained horses. The great Kelso ran in the International three years running and was beaten each time–by his compatriot T.V. Lark, by the French Match II in 1963 and by another American, Mongo. Finally Kelso won it in 1964 in a rip-roaring 2 mins. 23 and four fifths, a new American record for a mile and a half.

Laurel at International time is fun. Horses have come by train, plane and road from as many as 17 different countries on all-expenses paid trips. Around the specially created "International Village" in the stable area you can hear a dozen languages spoken, while the visitors gaze goggle-eyed at American training methods, and the locals see if they can trade some cigarettes for a Russian racing shoe.

What started as a promotion to aid an ailing racecourse has not only achieved that objective, but has helped to break down barriers in racing, so that the international exchange of runners and breeding stock has been accelerated, and colour added to an already colourful sport. Laurel, like other American tracks, has a hard working publicity department which pours out a mass of mimeographed material for distribution to press men. One well known racing writer told an amaz-ed English journalist visiting the Washington D.C. International: "Listen, if you want to go off and read a book or get stoned in the bar, when you come back you'll find everything you want–description of all the races, interviews with owners, trainers, jockeys or anyone else who happened to be around, weather forecast–the lot. And if you're too drunk to write your column even with all that, somebody'll help you out–though I wouldn't guarantee it every day of the week." In spite of the spoon feeding, American newspapers have a good share of columnists who produce amusing, individual comment on the racing scene and write with authority on racing and breeding.

Close to Laurel is Pimlico, home of the Preakness Stakes, the second leg of the American Triple Crown and possessor–until a tragic fire in 1966–of a superb old Members Clubhouse, built in 1870. Home now of the Maryland Jockey Club, which was founded in 1743, Pimlico has seen in its Preakness many of the horses which have made American racing history. The Preakness was, in fact, first run in 1873, two years before the Kentucky Derby, which precedes it in the Triple Crown.

Opened in October, 1870, Pimlico is the second oldest track in the country. While modern American presidents have tended to keep away from the races, possibly not wanting to endorse a gambling sport and thus upset the protestant vote, George Washington often went racing at this Maryland track, Andrew Jackson was a member of the Maryland Jockey Club, and President Lyndon B. Johnson went to see the Preakness several times before he became the occupant of the White House. Jockeyship is the theme of a permanent display at Pimlico, where the National Jockeys' Hall of Fame houses oil paintings of many of the country's outstanding riders.

And so across Virginia and West Virginia to the State of Kentucky, and Churchill Downs, a track which has more individual "character" than any other in America. Its twin spires dominating the centre section of the largely wooden stands are its trademark. When the Kentucky Derby was first run in 1875, 10,000 people attended the meeting on the outskirts of Louisville. Now the Louisville catchment area of racegoers, which has its local General Electric factory and division of the Ford Motor Company, stretches far beyond the circuit, and enthusiasts trek to Churchill Downs from all over America for the Derby. Record attendance on Kentucky Derby Day is more than 105,000. The stands have spread and sprawled to accommodate them, added to here and there through the years, and rattle emptily on a quiet day when there are merely 8,000 or so spectators.

Derby Day has an electric atmosphere all of its own, and good horses have lost their chance before the start through stage fright. As at Epsom, it requires a good horse to win the Derby, with the right temperament for the pre-race parade, the speed to hold his place in a race run flat out from start to finish.

Churchill Downs on Derby Day, always the first Saturday of May, is the centre of national attention. Press, radio and television coverage is enormous, a huge press box some 50 yards long accommodates writers from all over the States, bands play, crowds flock into the infield, seldom used for race viewing or picnicing on other tracks. After it is all over people go away and say "Why the hell don't they pull down that place and build a decent set of stands?", but the management know they have got something different to the average American track. The magic of the Churchill Downs atmosphere could well be lost in rebuilding.

At ten furlongs the distance of the Kentucky Derby is two furlongs shorter than the Epsom Derby, but it is still a tough gruelling race. The horse that wins the American Triple Crown has to be made of steel, for Pimlico's Preakness comes only 14 days later, and the third leg, the Belmont Stakes at Aqueduct is a mere 21 days further on. In fact there has not been an American Triple Crown winner since Citation in 1948, and only eight horses have won all three races in the history of American racing.

Seventy miles from Churchill Downs is the heart of the American thoroughbred breeding industry, Lexington, surrounded by the Blue Grass country. Some of the finest breeding farms in the world stand on a limestone outcrop where land is worth up to $3,500 an acre. Lexington today is no sleepy country town, and it has its own university and, like Newmarket, other industries apart from horse breeding. Neon signs flash in the main street, there are bars and ten pin bowling alleys. But outside the town there are miles of white railings and a concentration of top thoroughbreds in the paddocks beyond from all over the world. English, American, French and South American Derby winners stand on stud farms rich with mares and with yearlings being readied for the sales at nearby Keeneland or at Saratoga in August. On the ground floor of cool barns stand the equine produce of this rich land, and up above in the loft is a different kind of crop, tobacco, being prepared for auction in Lexington's long, low tobacco sheds.

Visitors are welcome on many Lexington farms providing they observe some commonsense rules. They can buy postcards and get maps and brochures. At one of the biggest farms, Spendthrift, which produces some 250 yearlings each season, more than 75,000 signed the visitors' book in one year. Visitors mean work, but Kentucky's big commercial breeders realise that it is the public who provide the prize money that justifies the prices their yearlings fetch at the sales, so they work at their own public relations.

Lexington has its own racetrack, Keeneland, a

From top to bottom:
55,000 people watching seven horses. Saturday afternoon at Aqueduct—the Big A—New York's mammoth track where some five million dollars are bet on such a day.
If you get behind in a race on a dirt track when it's been raining, this is the kind of view you get. Changing goggles three or four times in a race is one of the necessary skills for an American jockey in wet weather.
And this is what you may look like at the end of the race.

non-profit making operation opened in 1935, which provides a testing ground for the produce of the hundreds of stud farms in the area. The crowd at Keeneland is knowledgeable and if you want to look at horses there is plenty of opportunity in the pleasant paddock at the rear of the stands. If you just want to read about them, the Keeneland Association's Racing Library has probably the finest collection of racing books in the world, assembled under the loving care of Mrs. Amelia King Buckley.

Lexington is also the scene of a number of major sales conducted by the Keeneland Association and Fasig-Tipton Company of New York. American yearlings are sold standing still, unlike those of most European countries, where they are walked round a ring. The pace at which the auctioneers conduct their business under the floodlights is at first bewildering to a visitor. Spotters keep an eye open for bids and call them out to the auctioneer, who stops from time to time to harangue the audience about their lack of intelligence in letting such heaven-sent opportunities pass them by.

It was while one of these sales was going on that we slipped away to a block of stalls and saw what must be an unusual sight–two Kentucky Derby winner standing in adjacent stalls. One was the 1958 winner Tomy Lee, who was bred in England and after a distinguished racing career went to stud but failed to get any mares in foal and was returned to racing to win four races. Tomy Lee eventually went back to stud but never made his reputation there. In the next stall was Carry Back, who won the Kentucky Derby in 1961 for his owner, trainer and breeder Jack Price, and who was being "unwound" before going to stud. Jack Price had the courage to run Carry Back in the Prix de l'Arc de Triomphe in 1962 and the horse had finished 10 th. Price contributed a lively column to the racing paper The Morning Telegraph before and after the race which convinced many people that he had mistaken his vocation. Carry Back was one of those horses which from time to time capture the imagination and interest of a large number of fans, and the mail he received was only surpassed by that addressed a couple of years later to the great Kelso. The latter was honoured with his own wrapped sugar, and a book which could be obtained by writing direct to Kelso, Woodstock Farm, Chesapeake City, Maryland. This winner of just short of 2 million dollars and 39 of his 63 races for Mrs Richard C.DuPont had his own fan club (and so did Carry Back), his own mail box, prompted columns of poetry starting with lines like "Hail him, Americans. Stand up and shout your cheers, Bravo a true champion, the finest of our years". He also received letters

118

from all over America, including one which read "Dear Kelso, God put us here at the same time, you to be a great race horse and me to be a good boy for my mother and father. Good luck in 1965."

The world's most valuable race was at Chicago's Arlington Park, a vast establishment 12 miles from the world's busiest international airport, O'Hare. Here there is a nine furlongs dirt track, and inside it a superbly maintained turf course over which several American grass track records have been set. The richest race on the dirt course was, until its cancellation in 1970, the Arlington-Washington Futurity for two-year-olds, which was worth $385,350 to the winner, Strong Strong, in 1968, or about £160,700 if you want your cheque in English currency. Arlington boasts a strong programme of races on the turf in its programme of nearly 100 racing days between May and September.

Probably the most aggressive go-out-and-get-the-fans tracks in the world are California's Hollywood Park and Santa Anita which together give Los Angeles something approaching 150 days' racing, plus the 42 days allocated to nearby non-profit making Del Mar.

California's racing year really starts before New Year's day when luxurious Santa Anita opens on December 26 for a meeting that lasts some 70 days–providing the tote operators and other workers do not go on strike as they did in 1969-70 and completely disrupt more than a month's racing.

Santa Anita, is set against the background of the San Bernadino mountain range, with a midfield lake and tall palm trees. Breaking the conventionality of American race tracks is the undulating $1\frac{3}{4}$ m. turf course, which starts beneath the shadow of the mountains, and joins the main oval three furlongs from the winning post. This is the course on which was run the first race in America ever to carry $100,000 added money, the San Juan Capistrano Handicap, inaugurated in 1947, won in 1963 by England's Pardao, and in 1969 by France's Petrone.

When Santa Anita closes in early April, nearby Hollywood Park opens a few days later and continues until late July. Hollywood Park, too, boasts a fine turf course, and in 1970 offered turf prizes worth nearly £400,000. Film stars and Hollywood executives are often seen here, and president of the track is producer Mervyn LeRoy. Genial Executive Vice-President and General Manager James D. Stewart probably knows the world of racing as well as any American race track executive, and like Jean Romanet of France and a few others believes in the development of international racing.

Both Santa Anita and Hollywood Park maintain hard working publicity departments, and between them spend more than three million dollars on advertising. Hollywood Park's publicity men visit social clubs night after night exhibiting colour films of racing and answering questions about the sport, while their Railbirds Club, brings hundreds of fans to the track in the mornings to watch horses at work and to meet trainers and jockeys.

Californian racing during the summer centres on Del Mar, started in 1937 by a film world consortium headed by Bing Crosby and Patrick O'Brien. This attractive course, close to the Pacific Ocean, and with a tree-lined parade ring, makes big contribution to charities. Control of the track was transferred in 1954 to an organisation formed to fight juvenile delinquency, and while the track is leased to the Del Mar Turf Club, a quarter of a million dollars, or 90 per cent of the profits, whichever is the greater, is devoted to that cause every year.

When the cold winds begins to eat into the northern states in the Fall, the east coast racing scene gravitates south to Florida. Trainers, horses, grooms, work riders, hot-walkers, journalists, tele-type operators, tipsters and layabouts head for the sunshine and places such as Hialeah Park, twelve miles from the centre of Miami. Coral pink flamingoes delicately tip-toe through the infield lake as gamblers pore over the Daily Racing Form and the racing programme. Hialeah is surrounded by palm trees, the infield is a wildlife sanctuary, with many colourful wild birds besides the famous flamingoes, and there is an aquarium stocked with vivid tropical fish.

Tropical Park, opens in late November and continues to mid-January. Then Gulfstream Park and Hialeah take over. The Florida Derby, finishing against the background of Gulfstream's superb infield lake, has been the testing ground of many three-year-olds with classic hopes, and was won by three Kentucky Derby winners in the first ten years after its inauguration in 1952.

Florida boasts a growing thoroughbred breeding industry, centred on Ocala some 250 miles north of Miami. Here many of the big breeding farms of Kentucky now have annexes on rich land never previously used for the production of horses. Big money has been spent on stud buildings of advanced design, and an active Florida Breeders Association, with a well illustrated magazine, makes sure that as many people as possible know that you can breed racehorses in the state that was previously associated chiefly with holiday beaches, mangoe swamps, alligators and real estate sharks.

American racing is a vast, complex, multi-million dollar business. We have not even taken a look at diverse meetings such as Oaklawn Park in Arkansas; Northampton, Massachussetts; Turf Paradise, near Phoenix, Arizona; Monmouth Park, New Jersey, or 72 others.

The common denominator to them all is a realisation that to entertain people in this age of television and competition from a wide variety of participation recreations–sailing, roller skating, motor racing, golf–as well as spectator sports like baseball, and football, racing has to fight hard to hold its place in the market. You can *see* racing on an American track, the horses are never more than there furlongs away from you, and the publicity department of the track makes sure that as many people as possible know about the sport. There are plenty of problems within American racing, but at least it can claim to be an aggressive competitor in the entertainment business.

Canadian racing tries not to be an annexe of American racing, but the fact is that the two are inter-related.

Canada is a nation struggling for an identity. In Montreal the French influence asserts itself. England, centre of the now non-existent empire of which Canada was a part, tries to retain a hold, but all the time the American dollar asserts its influence–in racing as much as in any sphere.

Every summer, American horses come north to run in the best races in Toronto, the centre of Canadian racing. The best Canadian horses go south to compete for the top stakes in America. The only Canadian horse to win the Kentucky Derby was Mr E.P. Taylor's chunky home-bred colt Northern Dancer, who landed the Churchill Downs race in 1964. The sire of English Triple Crown Winner, Nijinsky, he now stands at an annexe of Mr Taylor's Windfields Stud Farm at Chesapeake City in Maryland.

Showpiece of Canadian racing is the Woodbine track, on the outskirts of Toronto, with a $15,000,000 grandstand, opened in 1956. Feature race here is the Queen's Plate, which is the oldest stakes race staged annually in North America. It was first run in 1859, and has been watched several times by members of England's Royal family, including Queen Elizabeth the Queen Mother, who visited Woodbine for the centennial running in 1959.

Woodbine is owned by the Jockey Club Ltd, which also controls Greenwood, close to the centre of Toronto, and home of the Queen's Plate from 1883 to 1955, as well as Fort Erie, modernised since its acquisition in 1952. Situated less than a mile from the United States-Canadian border, Fort Erie draws both on New York and nearby Buffalo for its patrons. A popular summer feature here is the Breakfast Club, which mixes trackside breakfasts for the family with track work, film shows and pony rides for the children. Canadian racing uses all the promotional techniques of tracks south of the border, and has made great progress as a spectator sport in the past two decades.

Punters weighing it up at the Big A

Lobbing to the start at Aqueduct

The car and the horse—two essential ingredients at a race track like Aqueduct

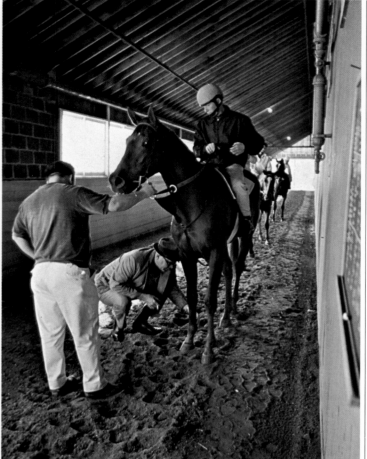

The moment for getting balanced and running –
a second after the start at
Hollywood Park.

"Skated in" on the dirt course at Aqueduct

Churchill Downs, Kentucky, provides facilities for most things, eating, drinking, talking, sleeping it off, making love. It also runs a horse race or two, including...

... the Kentucky Derby. Proud Clarion wins it in 1967 in front of a crowd totalling some quarter of a million.

After the show: runners for the last race at Churchill Downs head back to the race track stables

The Betting Man

What is racing about? Attempts have been made to allocate the very highest principles to horse racing. "The purpose of racing is the improvement of the thoroughbred," the English Jockey Club once said.

And what is the thoroughbred for?

Racing.

What it amounts to is that racing consists of a long series of differences of opinion, with everyone expressing his opinion in terms of money. When the whole thing started, Lord A. would bet that his grey mare was faster over four miles than Sir B.'s black gelding. Since then everyone has got in on the act. Not only are we all betting on the horses of people to whom we have never even been introduced, but we wager on animals in other states, other countries, the other side of the world.

True, there are people who go to the races just for the love of seeing these superb horses in action. We know a man who has walked round every racecourse in the British Isles. He knows every bend, every gradient. One day he was sitting in a train poring over past performances. A man walked in, whom we quickly identified as one of the boys who make their living playing cards with complete strangers.

"Fancy a game of cards?" he said to our innocent looking travelling companion.

"No thank you," said the latter, looking up and then returning to the form book. "I never bet."

"Do you hear that, he never bets and he's studying the form book like it was his bank account," we heard the wide boy complaining bitterly, as he went in search of more co-operative prey. "He must be nuts."

They *do* exist, these people who like horse racing and horses, but never bet. They may have been raised on a farm, love to see a thoroughbred in his natural surroundings, know him by his name, his outline against a green wood, not by a number on a parimutuel ticket. They do exist, but you will not meet them every day of the week.

It is the *betting* man to whom the gates of the modern hippodrome are opened. He bet 5,303,653,821 dollars in one year on American tracks, and probably as much again through the illegal books. He spends an estimated thousand million pounds a year on horse racing in Britain; one hundred million dollars in a year in New Zealand, with its tiny population. He is the man the track's board of directors, the publicity office, the caterer, the car park manager, the mutuel clerks, even the stewards at the meeting, are all trying to please.

What goes on in the mind of the betting man, this multi-billionaire to whom owners, trainers, breeders and jockeys must admit, however reluctantly, that they owe a lot?

After studying the betting man in Sydney and Siam, Bangkok and Brighton we have come to the conclusion that it is safe to make one or two generalisations.

Firstly, there is no herd instinct about the horse bettor when it comes to making a bet. Each man is an island. Weight of money may result in one horse starting at a shorter price than others in the same race, but the people who have bet that horse will all have taken their decisions independently.

Many like to keep the knowledge of what they are betting in a race to themselves, until after it is all over. Time and again, friends at the race track talk about the prospects for a race and go off to place their bets, thinking that each knows what the others are betting. Then, after it is all over, they discover they have all changed their minds.

We are not talking here about the stern, professional type of bettor, who often knows exactly what he is going to do before he reaches the track. Even he has a failing which is world-wide. Ask him how he got on at the races, and the worst he will admit to is that he "lost a little". This means that he had a shocking bad day. If he tells you he "just about broke even" it has still not been the sort of commercial venture that he would tell his wife about. If he says he "covered his expenses", he probably lost just a little.

The non-professional changes his mind about the horse he is going to bet for the strangest reasons. He walks up to the parimutuel windows prepared to take a ticket on No. 11 and the man in front of him, whom he does not like the look of, does just that, so he switches to another horse. On some tracks the mutuel windows are numbered, which can have a drastic effect on the numbers of the horse selected by the racegoer patronising them. It's window No. 11 and it's the second of the month, so the money goes on No. 22.

Or they back a horse because it is called Enid and it is Aunt Enid's birthday, or because the jockey's silks are composed of their favourite colours; because the first person they saw on arriving at the track was the jockey or the owner or the trainer, because the horse's name is Changeable, and that is what the weather man said.

Lady Munnings, wife of Sir Alfred Munnings, the great painter of racehorses, used to take her black pekinese everywhere with her, even to the races. When the horses were circling in the parade ring, the dog would sometimes bark. So she backed the horse that was passing at the time.

Actor Robert Morley has his own method. If he sees the owner surrounded by a pack of young children "on no account," he says, "back the horse. But if the owner is accompanied by a beautiful lady, not his wife, plunge to the hilt."

There was a man who worked in the sports department of a national press agency, and whose betting turn-over was alarming in comparison with his salary. However, he never admitted to anything more than having lost a little. He did all his betting with a bookmaker over the telephone, and got his results from the teleprinter, standing peering at it at race times, waiting for the first few letters of the winner's name to appear. He once had £100 on a horse running at Newmarket called Our Betters. The teleprinter started to tap out "Our B ... "

"It's won," he shouted, causing the racing editor to raise his eyes from his work and glare, as the punter went back to his desk.

A minute later someone pointed out that the teleprinter had gone on to print out the name of not Our Betters but Our Babu, a 20-1 shot. That was only the third race of the day. Our friend was like many others who think that each day is a separate unit, and that it is no good ending a day on the losing side. He battled on to back three more losers, and declared at the end of the afternoon, "I shall never wear this tie again. I last wore it at Ascot when Cyrus the Great got beaten at even money, and I had a feeling it might bring me bad luck."

He then left the office, carrying a rolled umbrella and wearing a bowler hat but no tie, to the amazement of the more properly attired business men on the electric train out to the suburbs.

We doubt if he were any more eccentric in his betting than a large percentage of the millions who flock to the race tracks, or bet by other means. It was just that he allowed his emotions to show a little.

As long as there is a possibility of big money being won in racing, the betting man will from time to time try to do something to influence the results of races.

In this he may occasionally be aided by an unscrupulous jockey with such equipment as an electric battery to impel his mount to greater effort, or with a particularly strong arm, which can make a big difference to a willing horse.

Sometimes, other outside influences are brought to work, such as happened at a small country meeting in England. When it was seen that the short priced favourite was well and truly beaten, some of the sporting gentlemen who had come down from the city to wager on the horse, rushed to the judge's box, which was little more than the sort of narrow sentry-box provided outside Buckingham Palace, and turned it over, trapping the official inside. He was released a minute later unharmed, but as the horses had already galloped past the post, there could be no official verdict, the stewards had to declare it "no race", and the boys got their money back.

One of the biggest gambles ever brought off on a racecourse was as the result of the conviction that the American trainer Max Hirsch had about the chance of a horse called Sidereal in a race at Aqueduct in 1924. He regarded Sidereal as an absolute certainty, and he and the horse's owner, a gambler named Arnold Rothstein, (depicted in the film "Funny Girl" by racehorse owner Omar Shariff) went to work on the bookmakers who in those days provided the only betting facilities at the New York track.

Usually when a man as shrewd as Max Hirsch went to the bookmakers and started betting on a horse, the price would be reduced rapidly. On this occasion the trainer and owner hit on the idea of asking a number of wealthy friends to place their bets. These were all people who would customarily have large bets on horses for no reason at all other than that they liked their chances, and thus when they placed huge individual wagers on Sidereal there was no suspicion that this was inspired money. They obtained odds of up to 40 to 1, Sidereal galloped to an easy victory, and the total that Hirsch and Rothstein collected was 770,000 dollars, or, in those days, about £192,000.

In England, probably the largest amount paid over one single bet went to the late Mr Bernard Sunley, the London real estate dealer, who collected £70,000 when Santa Claus won the Epsom Derby in 1964. He was also responsible for one of the largest losing bets ever recorded–that is largest in terms of the liability of the bookmaker if the horse had won. He struck a wager of £100,000 to £20,000 about his own horse Out and About in the Mildmay of Flete Challenge Cup at the big meeting at Cheltenham in March, 1964. Out and About was unplaced, so Santa Claus' win a few months later must have helped considerably to straighten out Mr Sunley's betting accounts.

Threequarters of an hour earlier another property owner involved himself in the biggest outlay on one horse that the writer has encountered, and it, too, was a loser. The occasion was the Gold Cup, the championship race of the year for steeplechasers, and it was the first occasion that the Duchess of Westminster's great horse Arkle appeared on the course at Cheltenham. Irish racegoers were amazed that English bookmakers offered them as much as 7 to 4 against him winning, while England's champion, Mill House, who had won the race the previous year, started at 13 to 8 on.

Betting booths on the infield at Longchamp, 1870 (above). Wherever you are, it needs knowledge, concentration, confidence, hard work and luck, to back winners—in Moscow or at Epsom.

That starting price was largely the result of the activities of one man, who, it was found after the race, had laid no less than £33,000 to £24,000 on Mill House with various bookmakers, and then had to watch him come in five lengths behind Arkle, who knocked four seconds off the track record in the process.

Another huge bet that went wrong was on a two horse race at Ascot. Royal Forest, ridden by England's greatest ever flat race jockey, Gordon Richards, had only to canter to the starting gate and canter back again to beat a very moderate opponent, but as the gate went up–it was in the days before starting stalls–he dug in his toes and whirled round, letting his opponent stroll home alone. Unfortunately, one regular racegoer laid £18,000 out to win £1000 on Royal Forest. It took him some time to work off his debt, but he can still be seen on the racecourse today studying the card and the form book and pitting his wits against odds, human nature and equine perversity. It takes a lot to change the habits of the betting man.

Concentration—Tokyo racecourse 1971

Paying out; and hoping for a pay-off, Palermo racecourse Argentina

Hope, despair and frustration at Aqueduct

South America and 75,000 Thoroughbreds

In the vast continent of South America, with its contrasts between civilisation and savagery, wealth and poverty, there are some 75,000 thoroughbreds, 80 race tracks in or near the teeming big cities, and probably the most volatile racegoers in the world. The atmosphere at a South American race meeting is charged with electricity. A result or a steward's decision which is not approved of by the crowd can bring an uproar of booing and whistling.

Some great racehorses have come out of South America, mainly to race in the United States, where trainers have increasingly become conscious of the potential of horses bred south of the Panama Canal. Numerically with the greatest potential for breeding good horses is Argentina, which has some 13,000 brood mares and about 9,500 horses in training, and indeed this country has been responsible for some real champions. Among them was Forli, who was unbeaten in Argentina and often won his races by a dozen or more lengths. Bought for a million dollars by an American syndicate, he won two races at Hollywood Park and an exhibition event, and then tragically broke a cannon bone in his left foreleg in a race at Arlington Park. He is now at stud in Kentucky.

Forli is one of a long line of good horses which have won Argentine's greatest race of the year, the Carlos Pelligrini over 1 m. 7 f. at the fine San Isidro racecourse on the outskirts of Buenos Aires. Racing here is on turf, but Buenos Aires' other course, Palermo, is a dirt track, and Forli laid claim to the title "South American Horse of the Century" by winning with equal ease in alternative races on both surfaces.

He sliced through the Polla de Potrillos, Argentina's equivalent of the English 2,000 Guineas, in 12 lengths in a South American record for a mile, won the second leg to the Triple Crown, the Gran Premio Jockey Club, and then, in spite of being off his feed, took the Gran Premio Nacional–the Derby–before going on to beat the older horses in the Carlos Pelligrini.

Forli, a son the English-bred Aristophanes, won good money but the average stake in Argentina is poor, and there is every temptation for owners to sell to the American trainers and bloodstock agents who come south looking for horses to compete for the good North American prizes.

A visit to Palermo racecourse reveals one of the problems facing Argentinian racing. There is no totalisator on the track, and betting has to be carried out by phone with a central office in the city. Betting has to be stopped ten minutes before each race to enable the tote organisation to balance its books, there are great delays in wagering, and sometimes the intervals between races are extended to 60 minutes so that bets can be placed. Illegal bookmakers thrive, and make no contribution to the sport.

Those conducting racing have for years been pressing for Government authority to proceed with a modern totalisator system. It will cost far more to instal now than it would have done when the idea was first mooted and squashed, first through lack of imagination and then through financial considerations and government interference during the Peron regime. Once the step is taken, Argentina with its many fine stud farms and a long history of importing the best stallions and brood mares from Europe that it could afford, will be in a position to stem the drain of its best horses to the States.

Brazil, the South American country with the second highest thoroughbred population after Argentina, has only a third of the number of horses, but the same problem–no totalisator. The population of Sao Paulo, where racing takes place at Cidade Jadim Hippodromo, grew from two millions to four millions between 1945 and 1960, but because no investment was made in a tote to ensure a proper reimbursement to racing from the betting turnover, the sport's income has been almost static against a background of rising costs.

Sao Paulo is just south of the Equator, but as it is 2,500 ft. above sea level it enjoys a temperate climate. The Jockey Club de Sao Paulo, housed in a magnificent building, has more than 7,000 members, and is able to maintain a stallion station, usually with seven stallions. The buildings are superb, and the standard of organisation set by the stud's supervisor, Dr Ulrich Reiner, is high. In a typical season 190 mares visit the seven stallions, and 85 per cent are got in foal.

There are laboratories, an operating theatre, and a staff of 110, including grooms, carpenters, mechanics, 56 bungalows for married staff, and a large dormitory building and restaurant for the single men.

As in Argentina and other countries south of the Equator, Brazil does not hold yearling sales. Horses are sold as two-year-olds, and they do not race before January, half way through their two-year-old season. For the top class Brazilian horses, and for others besides, there is a fair amount of travelling between Sao Paulo, and the capital, Rio de Janeiro, some 300 miles away, where racing takes place on the Gavea course. In fact there is a certain amount of rivalry between the two centres, with exactly parallel series of classic races being staged in both places, though not simultaneously.

Yet another country suffering from the lack of income from betting is Uruguay, where racing at Maronas on the outskirts of Montevideo is tremendously popular but the prize money appallingly low. As a consequence, any horses in training which show any promise are quickly packed off to buyers from Venezuela, Panama, the United States and Argentina. Average prize money for run-of-the-mill races in Uruguay in 1967 was about £75, which is hardly enough to keep the horses at home.

In Chile, the long land which stretches 2,700 miles down the Pacific coast and is nowhere more than a hundred miles wide, the Government has realised that if horses are to be exported to other countries, than at least efforts must be made to ensure good breeding stock, and has encouraged the importation of stallions and broodmares from Europe. There is a broodmare population of nearly four thousand–the third highest in South America–and 225 stallions at stud, many of them well known to the racegoers of England, France and Ireland.

The racing year opens with the summer meeting at Vina del Mar on the coast. This is a grass course while Santiago, to which the racing scene switches after the running of the St. Leger in March, possesses two tracks–the Hipodromo on sand, and the Club Hipico on grass.

It is in Peru and Venezuela that racing has reached a state of prosperity that one would expect in a continent where gambling and the lottery are so popular. These two countries have a tote monopoly, and the standard of prize money and racing amenities are far ahead of that in their neighbouring countries.

Lima, the capital of Peru, with a cool, refreshing climate, offers many entertainments besides horse racing at the Hippodromo Monterrico, including cock fighting, football, bull fighting, polo and surfing–though whether all these come under the heading of entertainment depends on how much blood you like with your sport.

Lima's Monterrico race track, a nine furlongs dirt course, is in a pleasant park in the foothills of the Andes. The Jockey Club lavished £2 m. on the course, with handsome grandstands holding 40,000 people, stabling for 1,500 horses, and bungalows and dormitory accommodation for trainers and men within the well appointed stable units, each housing some 30 horses. In 1967, the population of Lima was betting some £400,000 on 30 races each week-end, and racing was supported by a 16 per cent rake-off, a further 10 per cent going to the Government.

The trainers pay no rent for stabling or for use of the seven furlongs dirt exercise track, but they are levied £4 per head each week for their staff for their social security and health insurance. There is free veterinary advice, and owners pay the reasonable rate of about £24 per month to have their horses trained. An interesting touch is the weighing machine over which horses pass on their way to and from exercise. A number of trainers in America and Europe believe in checking on their horses' well-being by weighing them regularly but this is the first track known to have supplied a public weighbridge for the purpose.

Evening racing is no new phenomena in England, but in Peru, where the sun disappears in the evening almost like a light being switched off, the decision to stage evening racing meant the installation of floodlighting at the Monterrico track. Racing starts at 7 p.m., and ends at 11 p.m., and the £150,000-worth of electric installations flood the track and the stands in a blaze of light. As soon as the horses are in the starting stalls, the lights on everything but the track are dimmed and the horses leap out of the stalls to race round the band of light while the crowd roars. The dramatic effect and the heightened impression of speed that the lighting gives has brought a steady increase in attendances. To European eyes, it may seem rather like greyhound racing, but the Jockey Club have no reason to regret their investment in Monterrico or its lighting system.

La Rinconada, scene of Venezuela's international classic event, the Classico Simon Bolivar, has one of the world's most magnificent grandstands. It cost some £24 m., and is set among hills on the outskirts of the teeming city of Caracas. The occasional machine gun fire and bomb explosions (one in the hotel at which we were staying) did not spoil our enjoyment of a day's racing at La Rinconada, reached after a drive out from Caracas past thousands of decrepit shacks perched on sides of the valley through which the road runs.

The huge three-tier stands with an enormous cantilever roof, were designed by Arthur Froehlich, who also created the new Aqueduct and new Belmont in New York; Monterrico, and Hollywood Park, California. La Rinconada was alive with people, betting like fury, even though the total deduction from the tote pools is 39 per cent. This savage deduction is shared between local Government, the central government and the racing authorities. It does not seem to worry the average Venezuelan racegoer that the odds are stacked heavily against him. He enjoys his betting, and if anything happens on the track that he does not like, he is not backward in expressing his views.

The stands include a Hall of Fame, with paintings of winners of the Simon Bolivar, rest rooms, a gymnasium, turkish baths, and an oxygen room for those who feel faint at the altitude of 3,000 ft. —or the results of the races. Beyond the oval dirt track there are lavishly appointed training stables and grooms' quarters, a swimming pool for horses with bad legs, and a veterinary surgery equipped with electrically operated operating table, enabling the vet to place an anaesthetised horse in any position. Above the table are floodlights, still and movie cameras and television to record details of an operation.

Everyone at the races wants to win the Five and Six, a bet which you can also place the night before in many of the restaurants and cafés in Caracas. For the Five and Six, you must name the first six horses in the big race of the day, or get a consolation dividend by naming the first five. The odds against you are enormous, but everyone does it and dreams about the huge dividends. The deduction from this pool is even greater than that for the ordinary bets, but the man who lands a giant prize could not care less about how much went in taxes and towards racing if it enables him to move out of poverty and buy a lavish house in the best part of Caracas.

South Africa, a Flourishing Industry, but Isolated

When Van Riebeck and his pioneers landed at the Cape in 1654 there was just one horse, with a piece of rope halter on him, to be seen on the peninsula, and he was so wild that no-one could catch him.

Horses of one kind and another were imported into South Africa from that time on, but it was not until nearly 150 years later that the first race-meeting took place in South Africa. It was organised by the English settlers. The horses taking part in the early racing were thoroughbreds, augmented by imports from India and the East and even South America, together with local crosses.

The first race-meeting ever held in South Africa took place in September 1797. These early meetings were colourful events. The Paymaster General arrived on the course in an elegant curricle drawn by two white horses, and General Vandeleur in a fashionable gig. Lady Anne Barnard outdid them in a splendid carriage drawn by eight Spanish stallions, which, however, belonged to a wealthy Dutchman.

The carriages took their stations on either side of the winning post, stretching away in two lines of diminishing importance "the higher places appertaining to the carriages of the higher powers and exhibiting the beauty and fashion of the Cape." An observer noted "the regular graduation from the well-appointed English carriage to that curious piece of antiquity, the ancient Dutch–the gig, the light wagon cart and the long heavy wagon with its eight horses hired for the day and stuffed with black damsels in their brightest colours."

"There could be seen fashionable curricles, chariots, barouches with four horses, landaus, tilburies and dennets … The lawyers made the greatest display. The leading advocates came in barouches and four, the next in rank were content with curricles, while the notary followed in his solitary gig. Doctors turned out in chariots drawn by four greys, surgeons in barouches or tilburies, and the humble apothecary on his hack."

As was the custom at the time, races were run in heats. At the April meeting at Capetown in 1801, a race was run called "The 10-stone Purse of the

100 Pagodas". In *The Early History of The Thoroughbred Horse in South Africa* the author, the Hon. H. A. Wyndham recounts:-

"Two horses were entered owned by Colonel Dickens and Mr Muirson. The first heat was won after excellent running by Colonel Dickens' horse, and the second would also probably have been won by him if he had not bolted and thrown his rider. At the same time Mr Muirson's horse lost one of his stirrups and leather, by which accident the rider wanted weight when he came in; nor was the race decided in his favour till the shoes and nails of the horse had been included in the scale."

Today racing in South Africa is flourishing. In the early 50s the importation of foreign horses was prohibited for a period and there was fear that the homebred thoroughbred would be out-classed when overseas competition had to be faced. But when the ban on imported horses was partly lifted a few years ago, and horses with good form were brought in, the South African thoroughbreds decisively held their place. Indeed, when Colorado King, who was the outstanding three-year-old of 1962/63 was exported to the States, he continued to distinguish himself against American opposition, and won the Hollywood Gold Cup.

One great merit of racing in South Africa is that it is comparatively cheap. A good yearling can be obtained for around £3,000, and the cost of keeping a horse in training is only between £300 and £500 p.a.

Going to the races, too, is not expensive. Entrance to the Members' Stands at Turffontein near Johannesburg costs only about £1, and no introduction is necessary. Admission to the equivalent of the main ring in England costs only 25 p.

Starting stalls are now in use. The film used by the patrol camera is in colour, and is about the best in the world.

The climate of South Africa presents one of the principal difficulties. The racecourses are to-day well irrigated, and the going has more give in it than was the case a few years ago. Nevertheless the horses' feet tend to get dry and brittle. Stanley Gorton, one of the leading trainers, of Milnerton, Cape Province, has said he likes to shoe his horses a week before racing, and uses a mixture of cow dung and bran under the frog once a week to soften the foot.

Heat can also be a difficulty in moving the horses from one province to another, especially bringing horses from the Johannesburg courses 6,000 feet above sea level the thousand mile journey by train across the hot Karoo Desert down to race in the Cape.

Racing in South Africa is concentrated around the Cape, in Natal and in the Transvaal. There is little racing in the Free State. The Provincial

Shadows lengthen at the South African Turf Club course at Kenilworth.

Councils have received from the Government control of all sports, including racing, which they in turn have vested in The Jockey Club of South Africa. Taxation remains in the hands of the Provincial Councils, and differs considerably from province to province. In Natal they have off-course tote. At the time of writing, in the Cape there is no off-course totalisator betting, and bookmakers operate on and off the course at the Tattersalls' Clubs, but are not allowed to operate off-course on race-days, when only on-course betting is permitted. In the Transvaal bookmakers are allowed to operate on- and off-course on all weekdays, including race-days, while the totalisator is not allowed to operate off-course.

Racing flourishes particularly in Natal. The stakes range between £500 and £25,000. Though at one time handicaps were the most valuable races, and the Durban July, or £28,000 still is, the interest is shifting to classic races. Sprints are popular and most races are over a distance of between five furlongs and one mile. The premier handicaps are chiefly over one and a quarter miles, though the Durban—now the Dunlop—Gold Cup is over two miles as is the Chairman's Handicap in the Cape.

There are now about 3,000 horses in training. The principal Johannesburg racecourses are Turffontein and Germiston; at Capetown Kenilworth, Milnerton and Durbanville; at Durban Greyville and Clairwood. At Pietermaritzburg, Scottsville and at Port Elizabeth, Arlington and Fairview.

Each province has similar classic races—for example the South African Derby, which is always run on New Year's Day at Turffontein in the Transvaal; the Natal Derby, and the most valuable of the three, the Cape of Good Hope Derby, which is run at Kenilworth in late February, all over the Epsom distance of a mile and a half.

The circuit of the top-class horses is from the Transvaal down south to the Cape some time early in the year, and then in June (which is of course autumn) north to Natal for the climax of the racing year, the Rothmans July Handicap run over 1 m. 3 f. on the pear-shaped Greyville track, and in 1965 worth to the winner £28,000. It was first instituted in 1897, with a prize of £500.

"July fever" strikes the country around that first Saturday in July, and many who do not follow any other horse-racing would consider it unthinkable to let a July Handicap go past without a flutter. There have been times when its popularity caused grave discomfort and even danger to spectators. In 1918 the crowd was so great that they invaded the press Box and forced members onto the iron roof of the stand. It became known as the Rothmans July Handicap in 1963, when it was first sponsored by the tobacco firm.

Other valuable sponsored handicaps are the Benson and Hedges Metropolitan Handicap run over six furlongs at Kenilworth (Cape Town) and the Castle Tankard at Turffontein, Johannesburg.

No colours are better known on the South African turf than those of Mr and Mrs H. F. Oppenheimer, who have a stud at Mauritzfontein, Kimberley in the Cape Province. Many horses of their breeding have won for them, and they own Wilwyn, winner of the Laurel International for England, and a most successful stallion in South Africa.

South African racehorses are probably forever doomed not to participate in international competition because of the strict 60-day quarantine that other countries must impose in order to keep out the deadly African horse sickness, but horses such as Colorado King and more recently Hawaii II have shown that the country can produce top class runners. Hawaii, owned by the late Mr Charles Engelhard, who raced on a vast scale in South Africa, England, and America, won 15 of his 18 races in South Africa, including the Rothmans July Handicap, and went on winning in the highest class in America.

South Africa, with its apprentice riders' school, can also turn out good jockeys and has had no better ambassador for its racing, than young John Gorton, who was an instant hit when he visited England and as first jockey to Lord Rosebery in 1969 rode 72 winners.

India

Indian racecourses are among some of the most attractive in the world. Watered lawns and the green strip of the racecourse contrast with the sun baked ground around them, red and orange cannas grow in flower beds in the paddock, thousands of racegoers in white tunics and trousers, their ladies in bright sarees, fill the stands and mingle on the lawns.

It was the British Army that introduced organised horse racing into India, and the first recorded meeting was at Madras in 1795, though it is probable that racing took place before then. The Army raced mainly Arabs, but by 1847 when the Calcutta Turf Club was formed, sponsored by the merchants of the East India Company, thoroughbreds were being imported to the country for racing purposes and for breeding. In 1913, after King George V and Queen Mary had visited Calcutta, the Turf Club with its attractive white colonial-type stands was honoured with the prefix Royal. In 1960, Queen Elizabeth II, granddaughter of the royal visitors of 1913, and the Duke of Edinburgh, went racing there, and the Queen presented the trophy for the Queen Elizabeth II Cup, India's most important race, to the winning owner. Results of this race, which has at various times also been called the Viceroy's Cup, the Governor-General's Cup, and the King George VI Cup, show the impact of English and Australian riders on Indian racing, and never more so than in recent years. At least a dozen riders leave the shores of England as the fogs and frosts of late Autumn start and fly out to ride in India–and who can blame them. It is a far from arduous existence, with racing largely concentrated on the week-ends, and they return to Newmarket and Epsom fit and well for the start of the new flat season in March.

Bombay is the headquarters of the Royal Western India Turf Club, and its Mahalaxmi course is one of the sights of Bombay. A £50 race in November 1797, reported in the Bombay Courier, appears to be the first reference to horse racing in the area and it seems to have been a great success. The contest was followed by "break-fast for the ladies and gentlemen at the Race Stand, and a ball and supper in the evening". A few weeks later sufficient money had been subscribed for two such races to be run, with the first heat at 7.00 a.m. The day was a huge success and after the last race there was a 15 gun salute. What the horses thought of that is not recorded, but racing at Bombay was under way.

Mahalaxmi, first used in 1883, was in those days a dreary stretch of marshland, flooded in the

Calcutta racecourse, 1912. King George V, third from right, waits for the runners in the parade ring (above).
Nearly 50 years later, his grand-daughter, Queen Elizabeth II on a royal visit to India, sees English jockey Willie Snaith going out on Monkshood.

monsoon and dry and dusty at other times. The efforts of the Turf Club, which acquired the prefix "royal" after the visit of King George V (then Emperor of India) in 1935, have changed it into as pleasant a place to go racing as one could wish. It is the home of the Indian Derby, Oaks and St. Leger, as well as the Eclipse Stakes. A high standard of dress is still required in the Members' Enclosure, and a notice occupying two pages in the racecard states in bold type "The Authorities would be extremely reluctant to have to cause unpleasantness by having to refuse Members entry in to the Members' Enclosure on Race Days in case such Members are unsuitably attired. BUSH COATS, SHORTS, SHIRTS, AND TROUSERS WITHOUT COATS AND JEANS ARE NOT CONSIDERED SUITABLE ATTIRE".

In 1968 Bombay introduced off-course betting, to be followed later in the year by Calcutta, and there were indications that Indian racing, already climbing out of the doldrums of recent years, might go on to new prosperity. Balance of payment problems forced the Government to impose serious restrictions on the importation of bloodstock from overseas to inject new blood into the Indian breeding industry that from 1939 it had been the policy to encourage. As a result, there was a decline in the number of horses being bred, and the quality, and betting turnover was adversely affected. But in 1968, there was an increase in turnover, racecourse attendances and prize money, and a new record price was established at the annual yearling sales in Bombay.

Whichever way you look at it, the betting man is the most important ingredient in this particular sphere of sport–that is, after the horse. He bets, he wins or he loses, he picks his horses by all manner of means–astrology comes into it in India–but if he is given the facilities, and the government and the racecourses have organised matters sensibly, there is no reason why a racing industry such as that of India should not overcome its problems, make a healthy contribution to the exchequer and provide entertainment for millions.

Outside Calcutta and Bombay, racing takes place under the auspices of the South India Turf Club at Madras, Bangalore, Hyderabad, Mysore and Octacamund, and up in Darjeeling at the highest racecourse in the world. There, 7,000 ft. above sea level is the Lebong Racecourse, a tiny track known as the "Saucepan Course". A complete circuit is just over two furlongs, and the horses are locally-bred ponies, with an average height of 13.1 hands. The smallest and highest racecourse in the world, with the snow-covered peaks of the Kanchenjunga range in the distance, might not be Royal Ascot, but it is under Jockey Club Rules, and the sight of those diminutive Hyperions and Ribots tearing round Lebong's circular course, perched on the side of a hill on one of the few flat areas for miles around, is worth seeing. The occasional loss of one of the runners over the side adds to the fun.

Japan–a Power to Come

Nothing is more certain than an increasingly important place for Japan in the world of racing during the next decade. The dedication with which this country applies itself to anything which it considers important, its desire to absorb the best of industrial or social systems of other nations, and its ability to reject that which is uneconomical or regressive gives us the assurance that Japan will become a power in international racing within a short time.

In the past ten years Japan has imported stallions which won no fewer than twelve European Derbies, as well as classic and top-class winners of many other races. Every year delegations of Japanese owners, trainers and breeders arrive in Europe and scour the stud farms and sales rings for mares in foal and stallions. During the winter of 1969/70 alone, one international bloodstock shipping agency had to arrange six Boeing 707 flights each carrying between 18 and 26 valuable mares and stallions from London to Tokyo.

In the reverse direction, what has happened so far? Japanese ventures abroad with horses in training have not been successful, but at least they have had the courage to venture, and can be sure that better results are to come. The closest that any of their representatives in the Washington D.C. International in America has finished was the fifth of Speed Symboli in the 1967 race. Their Liverpool Grand National runner of 1966, Fujino-O, ran a game but hopeless race, jumping the huge fences with a courage which belied his stature. Japan has even sent a horse to run in Brazil. Hamatesso was flow to Sao Paulo in 1967 to run in the Gran Premio, and finished unplaced. The record looks rather sad, but anyone who has been around the sales rings and stud farms of the world in recent years must be convinced that all this will change.

Certainly at home, Japanese racing could not be in a healthier state. In fact, it is one of the few racing industries which is almost embarrassed by success. Japanese racing first became properly organised at Yokohama in 1861, but it was in 1888 with the introduction of the parimutuel and eventual governmental approval that the sport began to spread throughout the country.

The law governing horse racing changed a number of times up to 1954, when the Japan Racing Association was created, and the real growth period began. The Association, supervised by the Ministry of Agriculture and Forestry, has complete control of the racing, racecourses and the sale of parimutuel tickets.

This is yet another country where bookmakers are banned and as a consequence the racing industry is thriving and the state also draws a healthy amount from betting turnover. Deduction from the betting pools is 25 per cent, of which 10 per cent goes to the National Treasury and 15 per cent to the Racing Association, who must also pay half of their surplus to the Government at the end of each fiscal year after deducting all running expenses.

The Japan Racing Association controls five main courses–Tokyo, Nakayama, Kyoto, with its central lake and white and black swans, Hanshin, and Chukyo as well as five lesser tracks.

Some figures: record attendance at Kyoto is 70,506, at Nakyama 84,383, and at Tokyo 161,111. More figures: the total betting turnover in 1967 at racecourses and the Japan Racing Association's 14 off-course betting offices was 424,624,888 American dollars, and 22 computers were used to channel bets and calculate dividends.

In 1968 the betting turnover showed a 59 per cent increase over the previous year; in 1969 the total was up by a further 32 per cent, and the 1970 figure showed a further 26 per cent increase. The Government was becoming worried over the popularity of the sport, and a limit had to be set on the number of people attending each racecourse. Incredibly to other countries, no less than 95 per cent of the betting is on correct order forecasts–naming the first two horses to finish in their correct order. Horses are bracketed into groups, and providing the winner and second come from the two groups that you choose, you receive a dividend. In the off-course betting offices, lifts take the eager backers to the various floors: "First floor, win and place, second floor, forecasts".

The Japanese system of classic races for three-years-olds is much the same as that in England and France, with slight variations in distances. First comes the 1,000 Guineas, the Ohka-Sho Kyoso, for fillies, over a mile at Hanshin. The name of the race means the Cherry Blossom Prize, and the cherry is in full blossom when it is run. Nakayama, which has a tortuous steeplechase course in its infield, stages the 2,000 Guineas or Satsuki-Sho Kyoso, the first leg of the colts' Triple Crown races, in April and over 1¼ m. instead of the usual European distance for Guineas races of one mile.

Then comes the Oaks over a mile and a half for fillies, at Tokyo Racecourse, with its magnificent new and huge stands–the Yushun Himba Kyoso, about the third week in May. Traditionally on the last Sunday of May is the Japanese Derby, the Yushun Kyoso, again at Tokyo racecourse.

These races are all on turf courses, as is the final classic in the colts' Triple Crown, the Kikka-Sho Kyoso, or Japanese St. Leger, over 1 m. 7 f. at Kyoto. Once again there is a link between the race and the flowers that are at their best at the time it is run, for Kikka means chrysanthemum.

The classic races are open only to Japanese-bred horses. Prize money is well distributed within the industry, with trainers drawing 10 per cent, and jockeys 5 per cent plus a riding fee, and the winning stable also earns 5 per cent, for the stable lads. The breeders of winning horses receive one per cent of the purse. Stable lads' wages are strictly controlled, and the lads are members of a strong union. A recent increase brought the wages of a groom with long service to more than 10,000 U.S. dollars, or £4,000.

Besides the ten tracks controlled by the Japan Racing Association, there is a local racing association with responsibility for the registration of owners and horses, licensing of jockeys etc. in connection with racing on 32 minor courses.

The Japan Racing Association is a complex structure responsible for not only its ten race-courses, but for a number of ancilliary services. There is, for instance, the Utsunomiya Rearing Farm, where yearlings purchased from Japanese studs at various prices are raised. Owners ballot for the yearlings, and purchase them at the average price that the Association paid for them.

The Equine Health Laboratory section of the Association includes the Hot Spring Sanatorium at Joban City, a three-hour train ride north west from Tokyo. Here there is grazing land and exercise facilities, and tired or jaded horses or those suffering from neuralgia, rheumatism, external wounds or muscle, tendon or bone trouble can relax and take a restoring dip in the warm waters of a saline spring containing sulphur.

The Equine Health Laboratory itself is a large organisation making intensive studies of race horse diseases and hygiene, the prevention of race accidents, the improvement of environmental sanitation and racing performance. The pharmacology section deals with drug detection. Medication of horses was permitted in Japan until 1967 but it is now strictly controlled, and the first three horses in every race are tested for dope, plus any horse whose running is suspect. In 1968, there were eight positive cases, but in most of them the cause was found to be carelessness or ignorance on the part of grooms.

An important section of the Association is Equestrian Park, with its jockeys' training school. Of the approximately 200 jockeys riding on the major tracks, about half are products of this school, where the two-year course includes not only instruction on riding, stable routine, health, dieting, and rules of racing, but also schooling in ethics, sociology, the Japanese language, English, and the abacus. Equestrian Park's facilities include a race track, stables, dormitories for apprentice jockeys, a large parade-ground like riding area, and a horse show ground.

An applicant for a place in the jockeys' school must have had nine years of education, be 16 years old, weigh about 77 lb. (5 st. 7 lb.), and must be free of colour blindness and T.B. When he arrives at the school he is allocated his own room, and is issued with a pair of rubber boots, "riding uniform", leather riding boots, one summer and one winter working uniform, two pairs of cullottes, a two-piece rain suit, a thick wool sweater, a set of tools for grooming, and a whip. In addition to board, lodging and medical care, he receives five dollars a month. At the end of the course he must pass a stiff examination before being granted a jockey's licence. If he makes the grade and gets into the top half dozen in the jockeys' championship, he can expect to ride some 75 winners a year and earn some 11 million yen.

A look down the list of leading Japanese sires in 1968 gives some indication of the extent to which they have been shopping around for stallions. Champion sire was the now dead Irish Derby winner Hindostan, followed by Guersant from France, China Rock and Never Beat from England, Atrax and the King George VI and Queen Elizabeth Stakes winner Montaval from France, Die Hard and Solonaway from England and Hakuryo, bred in Japan and winner of the St. Leger and the Emperor's Cup.

The Emperor's Cup, incidentally, is run twice a year, once in the Spring and again on the official birthday of the Emperor in the Autumn.

One final statistic will demonstrate the flourishing condition of Japanese racing. In 1961 tote handled 37 billion yen. In 1970 the total bet was over 404 billion yen-ten times more than in 1951. With that sort of turnover they can afford to run their major races twice a year, and to look in wonder at countries with much longer racing traditions which are still struggling to organise the finances of their racing industries.

Palermo racecourse, Buenos Aires

155

Saddleless horses going out for a training session at Argentina's San Isidro racecourse

Dust is an almost essential part of the Palermo scene. Watering takes place between every race, but still the dirt track dries out and the runners reach the finishing line in a cloud of dirt.

159

Flying home with a jet trail at Palermo

Going out for morning work at Tokyo racecourse

Japanese racing attendances and totalisator turnover increase by nearly eight per cent every year. Limits have been set on the attendances at each track in the Tokyo area because of overcrowding in recent years. In this land-hungry city, the airport motor-way hugs the racecourse closely.

Australia—Eating, Sleeping, Talking Racing

Anyone who visits Australia at almost any time of the year without becoming conscious that horse racing takes place in that country must be lacking in one or more of his or her faculties. To be there at the time of the Melbourne Cup is rather like being in America at the time of a presidential election, except that the bars stay open on the big day. At about 2.35 p.m. on the first Tuesday in November, all Australia comes to a halt and glues its ear to a radio or finds a television set to catch every move in the event which has dominated the racing pages and forced its way onto the news and feature pages of the daily and Sunday papers for weeks.

To say that all Australians talk, eat and sleep racing is one of those generalisations which leaves out the tut-tutting spinsters who pull back their curtains to look at the traffic heading out of Melbourne for Flemington racecourse or the banner-carrying gospellers who parade near the track with their warnings in bright poster paints. But everywhere you go you hear racing being talked. "What's going to win the big one?" said the hotel doorman as we left for the course. "Well, you may be right but George Moore was in here yesterday and said that wouldn't live with the one he rides." "What'yre backing today?" said the cab driver during a commercial on his radio, breaking up an hour-long broadcast on racing. "Well, I wouldn't want that on my mind. When did a mare last win the Cup anyway? My old man said never back a mare in the Melbourne Cup and I ain't going to start now."

Melbourne Cup runners go to the post the most photographed big race contenders in the world. It seems an essential part of their preparation that they must pose for the cameramen together with local beauties, last year's Miss Australia, this year's Miss Victoria, the trainer's daughter, or the stable cat. Pre-race coverage of the race is enormous in the press and on radio and television, and is repeated on only a slightly lesser scale for the other big events in the Australian racing calendar.

A good way to start Melbourne Cup day is to call in at the Melbourne Museum to see the incredibly lifelike representation of Phar Lap, the horse who won the race in 1930 and a total of 37 races, who became a national hero, and whose death under mysterious circumstances after he had won a race at Agua Caliente at the start of an intended American campaign threatened to produce a severance of diplomatic relations between Australia and America. This is probably overstating the case, but his death, at first thought to be by poisoning but now accepted to have been through colic, plunged Australia into national gloom. Every vein stands out under Phar Lap's skin in his glass case in the Museum as he waits, seemingly ready to race for his life, looking out with clear eye over the heads of the continuous stream of people who come to pay homage to an Australian racing legend. Probably the performance which best illustrates his brilliance was to run in and win a seven furlongs race at Flemington a few outings after carrying 9st. 12 lb. to victory over 2m. He was odds-on for the 1930 Cup when someone tried to shoot him, and he was escorted to the racecourse by an armed police guard.

Melbourne Cup Day at Flemington is a day of pageantry. As the crowds begin to pour out to the course by train, bus, cab, car or helicopter, the massed Victorian Highland Pipe Bands are assembling ready to parade on the course. For the convenience of early patrons, the totalisator is open from 9.40 a.m. till 10.40 a.m. for betting on the Cup, says the 96-page programme. The Governor-General arrives in an open carriage, accompanied by the Horse Guards in black, people pause for "God Save the Queen" played by the Southern Command Band, and the stage is ready for the day's racing, with the first event starting at 11.40 a.m.

This is a day on which a number of members of the Victoria Racing Club, which owns Flemington, and visiting racing worthies, don grey top hats and morning dress. The occasional bowler hat can be seen, and the women really go to town with their dresses and hats. Indeed, many of the ladies never get to see a horse race for, as the programme announces, every woman and girl entering Flemington on any one of the four days of the Melbourne Cup Carnival becomes an automatic entrant in the "Fashions on the Field" contest. The prizes total more than £12,000 and include Ford cars, Qantas airline holidays in New York or New Zealand, trousseaux of Bri-nylon lingerie, evening gowns. Two sections of the contest are for ladies whose ensemble cost less than 50gns, or for more than that amount, there is a professional section for mannequins, models and designers, and a division for the most elegant hat. Judging goes on in all sections of the racecourse except the Members' Enclosure. There is also a "Quest to find the Best Dressed Country Racegoer", culminating in judging on the lawn close to where the horses are mounted in front of the stands, and the contestants are listed in the racecard, from

Warrnambool and Quambatook, Geelong, Ballarat and Wangaratta Turf Club. There are many photographers at the course, but not all of them are required to take pictures of the horses.

The densest gathering of humanity at Flemington is on The Hill, a huge uncovered stand looking down on the winning post, where thousands sit in shirt sleeves drinking beer and are not slow to voice their opinion on jockeyship, stewards' decisions or anything else which comes under the jurisdiction of a free, unbiased judge of the racing game. For a dollar you can buy a ticket from the Victorian Railways which gives you an electric train ride out from Flinders Street Station right to the racecourse, and admission to The Hill.

Costing about twice as much is admission to the Stand Enclosure, where you can reserve seats, and then there is the Members' Enclosure, with its subdivision of a ladies' stand. Racecourses in Australia and New Zealand have this interesting method of excluding the ladies from the members' stand proper, though the men can go into the ladies' stand and visit their wives and daughters if and when the fancy takes them. Thus the girls languish in their own stand and talk fashions and whatever else interests them in somewhat shrill voices which makes the ladies' section easily identifiable without looking when you walk down the length of the stands at Flemington, while all the time they are wondering how many scotches and beers the men are putting down in a bar which is inaccessible to them. It is a survival of the days when women were kept in their place, and racegoing gentlemen in England and America today wonder how the hell the Australians get away with it.

Behind the stands at Flemington are trees, big tote indicators, onto which all the off-course betting is fed before racecourse operations get going, a swarm of people, and the bookmakers in rows, their stands numbered and rigidly controlled by the racecourse, and topped by bright blue umbrellas to keep off the sun.

Australia has virtually abolished all off-course bookmaking by the sensible method of closing down their offices in town after town as and when the Totalisator Agency Board, established first in New South Wales in 1962, and spreading to all other states, became ready to open its own betting offices. The result has been that Australian racing has received a healthy injection of income from off-course betting, with, for instance an increase in money distributed by the T.A.B. to race clubs from the 1,016,183 Australian dollars in the first full year of operation ending in June 1966 to more than 2m. dollars in the year ending June 1969. Bookmakers are permitted to bet on the course, but it is not certain that they will be allowed to continue indefinitely.

Brunette Downs, Northern Territory of Australia, the stabling area and mounting yard are at their best in dry weather. That's about 364 days a year. The real inconvenience is danger of sunstroke or being choked to death by dust . . .
. . . contrasting the well populated and civilised areas of Caulfield, Melbourne, as the great Phar Lap, wins the Melbourne Cup.

The Melbourne area is well endowed with racecourses, for besides Flemington, there is Caulfield, operated by the Victoria Amateur Racing Club. With its mellowed, ivy covered stands, this is the scene of the mile and a half Caulfield Cup, first leg of the Caulfield–Melbourne Cup double on which many thousands of dollars are wagered. Also within easy reach of the centre of Melbourne is Moonee Valley, a tight nine furlongs circuit with a one furlong straight, demanding, as do most Australian courses, a high standard of jockeyship; and the latest track in Australia, Sandown Park, which opened on 1966 and includes a motor racing track in its facilities.

Victoria has its own set of classic races–the Caulfield Guineas, the Victoria Derby, the Oaks Stakes, and the V.R.C. St. Leger, run at Flemington, and so too does the state of New South Wales, where the principal track is Randwick, established in 1833. The Australian Jockey Club came into existence here in 1842, and gives its name to the A.J.C. Derby and other classics.

The houses of the suburbs of Sydney completely surround Randwick which, besides acting as a racecourse, is also the training ground for hundreds of horses, some stabled in blocks recently built on A.J.C. property adjoining the track and some in private stables in the suburban side streets around the track. In the early morning the racecourse, with its infield training gallops and special exercise track presents a lively scene as long strings of horses file out from the nearby stables.

Sydney is served by three other courses–Warwick Farm, which also comes under the jurisdiction of the A.J.C., and Canterbury and Rosehill, owned by the Sydney Turf Club. No one need ever go short of his racing in the urban areas on the east coast of Australia, for Brisbane, 600 miles north of Sydney, has three major courses, Doomben, Albion Park, and the senior course, Eagle Farm, headquarters of the Queensland Turf Club. Eagle Farm boasts a fine modern stand, named after Dr John Power, chairman of the Q.T.C., who aided in its design with the aim of getting as many of the public as possible near the finishing line. The public are on the upper deck of the stands, with the committee and members on the lower levels. As in Sydney, many of the local trainers live within easy reach of the Eagle Farm course, in a suburb called Ascot, and have their horses led from their yards each morning through the city streets to work on the course.

Outside Melbourne, Sydney and Brisbane, the chief racing centres are Adelaide, where the South Australia Jockey Club, founded in 1856, operates the Morphetville course, and Perth, where the name Ascot crops up again, home of the Western Australia Turf Club.

Four thousand miles separates racing in Perth from that on the east coast of the continent, and there is little interchange of jockeys and horses, though from time to time, Western Australia throws up a really good horse. Though foaled in New South Wales, in 1916, Sir Ernest Lee Steere's Eurythmic did all his racing in Western Australia, where he won all the main races before going east to carry on his successes.

But Australian racing is like an iceberg. The tip of the iceberg that shows in the record books is represented by the major tracks. Beneath that are the small racing clubs. Almost every town of any size in Australia has its own race track–some 700 in all, with more than 3,500 race days.

No visit to Australia is complete without a day at one of the "picnic" meetings, like Coonamble, 500 miles inland from Sydney, on flat, dusty land. A tent serves as the committee luncheon room, the two diminutive wooden stands hold about 200 each, but the attendance is usually about 3,000–not counting the flies. But in spite of a temperature in excess of 100 degrees and the primitive conditions, this is the Royal Ascot of the Coonamble district. Everyone dresses in their best, and the ladies all wear hats. The racecourse commentator, jammed in the stands so that he can hardly raise his binoculars, keeps up a patter which would have had him expelled from the job at Royal Ascot: "Here we go for the fourth race. The horses are just being put into the stalls. There's a fat man in stall number 3. I don't know why...."

The biggest prize at this meeting was £1,000, and it attracted runners from Sydney, who took the first two places, but this was exceptional for a country meeting. At the other end of the scale you have meetings like the Nowra and District Picnic Race Club in New South Wales, where the top prize was £30, and most of the races were worth £6 to the winner. Final race was the Beaten Stakes for horses that did not win the first five races.

Besides purchasing many horses from New Zealand, Australia is yet another country which has to continually return to Europe, and in particular to England and Ireland, to replenish its racing stock. Of the top ten sires of winners in Australia, it is quite usual for every one of them to have originated in Europe.

Chief breeding area is the Hunter Valley in New South Wales, and the largest stud there is Lord Derby's Woodlands Stud, where in recent years have stood the British stallions Pipe of Peace, Sostenuto, Sweet Moss, Rhythmic Light, My Heart and Chantelsey. In fact, a tour of Australian studs gives the European racing enthusiast an opportunity of meeting again many horses that he has seen in action on courses 14,000 miles away.

Not far from the Hunter Valley is the pictur-

A dignified Melbourne race crowd resting in the shade on a warmish day around 1905. Flemington racecourse, Melbourne, about 1890.

esque Widden Valley, with hills towering above the flat paddocks on the valley floor. The 4,000 acre Widden Stud, owned by Mr Frank Thompson is one of the oldest studs in Australia. Its stallions include Todman, twice leading sire of two-year-olds, and Vain, winner of 12 of his 14 races. It also keeps 800 of the massive Santa Gertrudis cattle, imported from the King Ranch, Texas. Here, on a sweltering day, we met veterinary surgeon Murray Bain, whose "parish" covers a vast area around his headquarters at Scone, where there is another colony of stud farms. As the temperature climbed into the hundreds again and the flies ignored the repellent aerosol we had hopefully sprayed on, we visited the attractive Oakleigh Stud, further up the Widden Valley, and saw more English stallions, Regal Light, Gaul and Red Gauntlet.

In the breeding areas, the backroom of Australian racing, life can be raw. At the end of a three year drought period, we drove past hundreds of corpses of sheep. When our vehicle sustained a puncture miles from anywhere, the huge black bird which came to perch on the telegraph wires to keep a vulture-like eye on us made us glad when the driver had completed his repair job.

If Australia imports stallions consistently from Europe, she also has one export which has had a notable effect on the racecourses of the world, and in particular England, Ireland and France –jockeys.

Since Frank Wootton went to England from Australia in 1908 and had such success in the saddle, Australian riders have had increasing impact on European racing and never more so than in the past 25 years. The French, English and Irish form books are studded with victories of men who were well known on the racecourses of Sydney, Melbourne and Brisbane, became household names 14,000 miles away. George Moore, Bill Cook, Scobie Breasley, Edgar Britt, Neville Sellwood, tragically killed in a riding accident at Maisons-Laffitte, Rae Johnstone, Jack Purtell, Brownie Carslake, Ron Hutchinson, Bill Pyers, and many more.

Some failed to fit into the European scene, did not make the grade in the early months after their arrival, and went home again, but the instinctive jockeyship of most of the Australians soon put most of them on the map.

The Australian method of riding exercise gallops against the clock installs in work-riders and jockeys an invisible mechanism which tells them when a race is being run too fast or too slow. The tight Australian circuits, usually with a run-in of about two furlongs or less, mean that the jockeys have to be quick-thinking and conscious of the need to save every inch of ground. Not all Australian jockeys are attractive to watch in a finish, and some do not appear to get as much out of a mount as a European jockey with a more dramatic style. But a rider such as the now retired Scobie Breasley had his horse in the right place at the right time, and if it was good enough to win it did. Certainly Australian jockeys have been a fine advertisement abroad for a progressive home racing industry in which good horses, good jockeyship, and a sound financial set-up are the main ingredients.

New Zealand

Eight hundred miles north and east of Australia lie the twin islands of New Zealand. You feel some of the remoteness from the rest of the world–the impression that you are living on the *edge* of the world–that seems to be present with many inhabitants of this delightful country, when the owner of one of the leading stud farms suddenly stops in the middle of showing you some brood mares and points to the east: "The sea is three miles that way, and after that the nearest land is South America," he says. "And that way, the nearest is Japan."

Horse racing occupies almost as important a place in the life of New Zealand as it does that of Australia, and it also makes a substantial contribution to the country's economy. In fact it is in much the same position in relation to Australia as Ireland is to England. Its stud farms produce a high percentage of the winners of big races in Australia. Of the ten Melbourne Cup winners between 1960 and 1969, no fewer than eight were foaled in New Zealand.

Phar Lap, one of the horses who has qualified for inclusion in the Twelve Best Horses of the past century in this book, was bred in New Zealand, and so was Tulloch, who was the dominating factor in Australian racing in 1957, and rated one of the best three-year-olds for many years. One writer commented on Tulloch, "Perhaps it is not parochial to emphasise that the colt has developed and matured in Australia since he was bought in New Zealand as a yearling, that he is the product of Australian training methods, is owned in Australia, and in all respects other than the country of origin is an Australian racehorse." We consider it was pretty parochial, but this sort of attitude has not had the slightest effect on Australian owners and trainers, who return year after year to the big yearling sales in Wellington in January. Of the 400 lots sold at the 1968 sales, for instance, 279 went to overseas buyers, including 234 to Australia.

A time could come when New Zealand thoroughbreds will have an even wider influence than they do at present. In 1968, Mr Geoffrey Rickman owner of the Bookham Lodge Stud in Surrey, England, visited New Zealand and purchased the stallion Cracksman, winner of the Great Northern Derby and the New Zealand St. Leger, and shipped him back to England. The New Zealand horse Terrific is now also at stud in France. Americans, too, are showing increasing awareness of the potentialities of the New Zealand horse, climate and soil, and millionaire Mr Nelson Bunker Hunt, who is building up one of the world's largest racing empires, recently purchased a stud farm at Matamata in the north island of New Zealand.

The principal track in the South Island is Riccarton at Canterbury but enjoyable though the racing is in this part of the world, visitors generally find the scenery of better quality than the standard of the horses.

It is in the North Island that the best New Zealand racing takes place, and particularly at Ellerslie, on the outskirts of Auckland, and at Trentham, just outside Wellington.

We were shown round the Ellerslie course by Dr A. McGregor Grant, then president of the Auckland Racing Club, whose colours were carried on New Zealand tracks for more than half a century, notably by the now exported Terrific, and whose 80th birthday in 1967 was celebrated by a dinner of tribute and a special race meeting at Ellerslie.

It was 1840, only 47 years before Dr Grant was born, that New Zealand racing, introduced by English settlers, really began to make strides, with the importation of the first thoroughbred stallion, the Australian-bred Figaro.

There are records of a race meeting which took place the year after Figaro was imported, on the beach at Wellington in the days when New Zealand's capital was not much more than a village of wooden shacks. The Clerk of the Course was expected, among other things, to extract boulders from the beach, get the dogs tied up and pigs removed from the course.

It was in the 1860's that New Zealand racing became properly organised with the establishment of racing and trotting clubs supervising the sport in the various districts. The Canterbury Jockey Club, which holds its meetings at Riccarton on the outskirts of Christchurch, instituted the New Zealand Derby in 1860, and though it tends to be overshadowed by richer stakes in the North Island nowadays, it has been won by many of the best horses to race in New Zealand.

Ellerslie was opened in 1910 by the Auckland Jockey Club and today boasts superb stands, modernised in 1954 and giving a fine view of the picturesque course. Most valuable race run here is the two miles Auckland Cup, staged at the January meeting and worth 30,000 New Zealand dollars, or about £15,000 and open to three-year-olds and upwards. In contrast the two classic races run at Ellerslie, the Great Northern Derby and the Great Northern Guineas, are worth only 10,000 dollars (£5,000) and 8,000 dollars (£4,000) respectively.

Ellerslie is a fairly sharp right-handed circuit. There is also a gruelling steeplechase course on which the Grand National is run. The course includes a stiff hill on the far side from the stand, to be climbed three times in the National, and a variety of jumps.

Headquarters of the New Zealand Racing Conference, the sport's controlling body, is in Wellington, at the southern end of the North Island. Though New Zealand supports a population of only three million, the strength and popularity of racing is indicated by the fact that there are no fewer than 89 racing clubs represented on the Racing Conference, with some 270 days' racing, and this does not include the 47 trotting clubs, who have their own Racing Conference in control, and over 130 days of harness racing. There are usually some 3,500 horses in training compared with about 11,000 in England and Ireland, where the population is about 18 times as great as that of New Zealand.

Racing at Wellington is centred on the superb racecourse at Trentham, where the year's richest races are the 31,000 dollars Wellington Gold Cup, (the biggest prize in New Zealand racing), the Wellington Derby over a mile and a half, and the George Adams Handicap over a mile.

Trentham is a course which was way ahead of its time when its magnificent stands were erected in the 1920s. With cantilever roofs, giving an uninterrupted view of the racing which takes place against a backdrop of rolling hills, the stands make one wonder just how much progress we have made in the design of racecourses over nearly forty years. This is not to minimize the work done recently by Arthur Froehlich of America, who designed among other stands the superb La Rinconada in Caracas, or Howard Lobb of England, responsible for the excellent stands at Newcastle. But in 1924 they erected stands at Trentham which would be an asset to any racecourse today, and which certainly were well populated on the day that we enjoyed racing there. A brass band played on the lawn between the two main stands, two tanker lorries were drawn up at the rear of the ivy-covered buildings, pumping cold beer to thousands of thirsty racegoers, and in the main stand an official sat assessing the situation at the totalisator windows in the last few minutes before a race. It will probably shock some of those who organise racing in other countries that the start of a race in New Zealand can be dictated by the number of people still queueing at the betting windows. The horses may be walking around behind the starting stalls for several minutes before the official decides that the time has come to stop betting operations.

The prosperity and growth of racing in this country lies in the fact that in the 1920's the government decided to do what almost every major racing country in the world except England has done and abolished bookmakers, so that off-

Programme

Maori Race Meeting
Karioi, January 1st, 1870

COME! COME! COME! NOTICE TO ALL!

This notice is to all friends in the East, in the West, in the North, in the South.

OH, FRIENDS LISTEN!

Horse races will be held at KARIOI.

These races will be run under the patronage of the King of Maori people.

STEWARDS OF THE RACES:

Chairman: Te Wheoro and his friends.
Judge: Te Tahuna and his friends.
Starter: Te Harihari and his friends.
Clerk of the Course: P. Wanihi and Te Amaru.
Clerk of Scales: Te Kamanomano.
Handicapper: Tom Pepa and his wife.
Treasurer: The Rev. Hori Wirihani
Secretary: Mrs. Harihari.

RULES OF THESE RACES:

1.—Men owning horses and wishing to enter them must deposit money in the hands of the secretary.

2.—Don't bring any drink to these races.

3.—Men who have taken much drink will not be allowed on this course. If any man disobey this rule he will bring the whip of the club down upon him.

4.—No girls will be allowed to ride as jockeys in these races.

5.—Jockeys must wear trousers in all events.

6.—No jockey must knock any other jockey off his horse or touch the reins of any other jockey or strike any other jockey with his whip during a race, or strike any other horse other than his own, or swear at or threaten any other jockey.

7.—Any jockey breaking these rules will be driven from the course if he does not pay twenty shillings to the treasurer.

8.—You must not change the name of the horse. You must not suppress the fact of a win at any other race meeting. You can be expelled or fined not more than 50s. if you break this rule.

9.—Persons allowed to see these races must not say rude words to the stewards, or swear at jockeys who do not win, or otherwise behave improperly.

A close finish—between the tide and the portable judge's stand at Castlepoint's beach meeting in New Zealand.

course betting would make a proper contribution to the sport on which it thrives. Those who say that England is different and that the betting public would never stand for tote only betting might just pause and look at what happened in New Zealand in 1922, when the population of that country was even more closely linked with family ties to England than it is today with immigrants of many countries changing the population pattern. A whole new generation has grown up in New Zealand which never knew what a bookmaker was. They flock to their big city racecourses, their country meetings and their "picnic" meetings in thousands, and no one misses the so called "colour" provided by the bookmakers on the course–probably the most expensive colour that any entertainment industry has ever tolerated.

Up to 1951, the only legal betting in New Zealand was on the totalisator on the racecourse, but the formation that year of the Totalisator Agency Board has had a marked effect on the prosperity of racing–and the income of a well informed Government which is aware of the need for a healthy goose that lays the golden eggs. Illegal off-course betting with bookmakers has been virtually eliminated, and the T.A.B.'s cash betting offices now pump a healthy 3.5 m. dollars into racing and trotting as well as to the Government. If these figures are applied to England, with its population of 55 million, racing there today would be receiving some £30 million (much the same as in France), and facing up to the challenge of those countries which at this moment are in a position to attract the cream of our runners and our blood lines. Perhaps New Zealand, where racing started some 300 years after it did in England, can still teach the home country a lesson which we will heed before it is too late.

A day's racing that we enjoyed as much as any during a world tour of racecourses was a blue-skied visit to Rotorua, home of the famous geysers and hot springs. We drove into town in a coach piloted by an ex-steeplechase jockey, Garry Du Loup, who took his vehicle over twisting mountain passes with all the dash of a man for whom three miles over fences on an inexperienced five-year-old would hold no fears at all. There were those in the party who just could not face sitting in the front seat as our pilot thumped his coach into a lower gear and took it down through endless hairpin bends, with a fall of several hundred feet on one side.

As you drive into Rotorua you can smell the sulphur in the air. The wooden stands on the racecourse are gradually being replaced by concrete structures with the aid of the grants that the country meetings receive from the T.A.B., losing perhaps some of their character but providing the facilities that the modern spectator expects.

The course at Rotorua is tight and jockeyship counts for a lot on the sharp turns, where racing two horses wide from the rails can mean giving away a lot of ground. The racecard was full of horses sired by horses imported from England. For some reason that no one has yet satisfactorily explained to us, New Zealand and Australia must continually return to Europe to replenish their thoroughbreds and their cattle, who tend to grow coarse and lose their quality without fresh injections of blood. There was a good crowd and a great feeling of local participation, for racing in New Zealand is everyman's sport, with local businessmen and syndicates of office workers breeding and racing their own horses, and hoping for one good enough to run in the major races at Wellington, Auckland or Christchurch. Long may it thrive, for New Zealand racegoers are as knowledgeable as any in the world, the sport is on a sound business footing, and they *enjoy* it.

Melbourne Cup runners returning to unsaddle

　　　　　　　　Caulfield

The carnival that is Melbourne
Cup day—fashion parades, hat
competitions, bagpipe players,
champagne and fish dishes, a
bride who couldn't miss this day
at the races. Somewhere there
might even be a horse.

Baghdad Note, Melbourne Cup winner, coasts up on the outside of the field

Ellerslie, Auckland's premier racecourse.

A field sets out on the flat course at Ellerslie

The Jumping Game

All horse racing is a difference of opinion, said Damon Runyon, and all steeplechasing is a difference of opinion on the respective ability of horses to get from one place to another at racing pace while negotiating a series of obstacles. It is a form of horse racing that can be seen in almost every country where racing takes place, but the importance of its position in the racing scene varies enormously from country to country.

It is always dangerous to assert that "The first steeplechase took place at X in the 17th century" because someone immediately writes to you with the claim that the Red Indians are known to have held jumping races a hundred years earlier. Indeed it is highly probable that ever since man tamed the horse and threw a leg over him, challenges have been made which have involved galloping and jumping.

It does seem, though, that modern jump racing originated in pounding matches in Ireland, in which one horse literally pounded his opponent to a standstill in a contest across the roughest stretch of country that could be found. One of the early matches recorded was between Mr Edmund Blake and a Mr O'Callaghan from the church at St. Leger in Co. Meath to Buttevant Church, with the steeple of the latter acting as a guide. This was the origin of the word steeplecheasing. But it was not until some 40 years later that steeplechasing matches began to be recorded in England. In 1810 the first proper course over three miles and eight fences was constructed at Bedford and in 1830 came the St. Albans Steeplechase, organised by the man who did more than any other towards spreading enthusiasm for steeplechasing. This was the owner of the Turf Hotel at St. Albans, Thomas Coleman, many of whose horses were ridden by Captain Becher.

One of the meetings at which Captain Becher rode was Maghull, on the outskirts of Liverpool, organised by a local landowner, Mr John Formby. However, a rival committee under Mr William Lynn, who owned the Waterloo Hotel in Liverpool, established races at Aintree in 1829, and seven years later advertised the race which was to be the predecessor of the Grand National. It was won by Captain Becher on a horse called The Duke, and was a great success, drawing a huge crowd, many of the people using telescopes so that they could see all the running.

The success of the race encouraged Lynn to stage in 1836 the race which came to be recognised as the first Grand National. This had £100 added prize money and was run "over a country not exceeding five miles, to be chosen by the Umpire or such other persons as he may appoint ... the ground to be shown to the riders on the morning of the races ..." Captain Becher missed the race as he was riding the previous day at St. Albans, and there were no trains, planes or motor cars to get him to Aintree in time. The Duke was ridden by a young Welshman, Mr Henry Potts, and won from three opponents. Among them was a horse called Zanga, who is noteworthy in that he was the first of many horses to fall in a Grand National.

Some of the records show that the first two Grand Nationals, 1837 and 1838, were run on a course at Maghull. In fact, Maghull races ceased in 1834, and the 1837 and 1838 races were staged at Aintree, though during the course of the race the runners did stray into the neighbouring parish of Maghull.

The next year the course was shortened and remained within Aintree, and the increasing popularity of steeplechasing is reflected in the fact that there were 18 runners. It was the year in which the race went to that most appropriately named of all Grand National winners, Lottery, and in which the gallant Captain christened Becher's Brook when the horse he was riding gave him a bad fall at what was described as "a high hedge, bank and rails, on the other side of which was a piece of water, let in for the purpose, full fifteen foot wide."

Stone walls, a stretch of plough, and a great variety of other obstacles, constituted the Grand National course in those days. The plough and one hurdle were included in the course right up to the 1920's but today the fences, though big, are more standardised, and modifications made on the take off side in 1962 have considerably reduced the number of fallers. Until then, there were seldom more than seven or eight finishers in a field of 30 or 40, but today it is common for 17 or 18 to complete the course.

Even if some of the sting has been taken out of the course, it still remains Europe's supreme test of horse and rider–four miles and 856 yards to be covered at an average speed of 28 m.p.h., 30 fences to be jumped, measuring up to 5 ft. 6 inches, a run from the last fence to the winning post of nearly 500 yards to finally test the courage of a tiring horse.

Incidents occur at Aintree that seem to happen on no other course. There was the case of Mr Anthony Mildmay (later Lord Mildmay), who was winning the 1936 race on Davy Jones when the reins broke between the last two fences and the horse ran out. There was Zahia who had the

The Windsor Grand Steeplechase. In the background of this now abandoned racecourse are Windsor Castle and the chapel of Eton College.

Grand National sewn up when his rider mistook the course on the run-in and threw away a chance that seldom comes to a jockey more than once in a lifetime.

There was that incredible finish to the 1956 Grand National, when the whole of Aintree was cheering to victory Devon Loch, owned by one of National Hunt racing's greatest supporters, Queen Elizabeth the Queen Mother. Thirty yards from the winning post Devon Loch suddenly pricked his ears, appeared to make half a leap and then sprawled on the ground, leaving E.S.B. to pass him and win the race. Many theories were put forward—that Devon Loch's metal shoe had struck an underground electrical cable, that he was startled by the noise of the crowd, that he suffered some form of muscular cramp. Having recently seen again the film of the finish, the author's view is that Devon Loch, gallantly ploughing through the mud up the long run-in suddenly saw the wings of the water jump on the parallel course and thought he had to jump yet again. The dumb misery of his rider Dick Francis, who leant on the rails and cried after Devon Loch had skidded to a halt, must have been one of the blackest moments that anyone has ever experienced in sport.

Modification of the fences has not removed that special Aintree drama. In 1967, a loose horse ran across the field at the 23rd fence, bringing down half a dozen others. Horse after horse galloped into the growing melee of fallen animals and jockeys until the complete race had been brought almost to a standstill. Then the 100-1 chance Foinavon, who had been toiling along at the rear of the field threaded his way through the turmoil and went on to win from a string of horses who had been remounted and had set off in hopeless pursuit of the one horse on whom the Gods of Aintree had smiled.

Aintree occupies so much space in this chapter because the name "Grand National" has had such influence on steeplechasing throughout the world, and almost every country where jumping takes place has its own Grand National. Yet if one had to name the true home of English steeplechasing, it would not be this mouldering giant of a race-course, surrounded by railway sidings and factories, with a range of grandstands into which the Topham family, who own the course, can hardly be said to have poured loving care and attention over the years.

The true heart of jumping, with its 46 courses of varied attractions throughout the country, lies at Cheltenham, where against the superb backcloth of the Cotswold Hills, championship races such as the Cheltenham Gold Cup and the Champion Hurdle are run. Cheltenham, owned by the non-profit-making Racecourse Holdings Trust, now has two completely separate two miles steeplechase courses, an enormous advantage when one or other course takes a hammering from hundreds of pounding hooves in mid-winter. Combined, the two courses give the necessary distance for amateur riders' marathons such as the four miles Fox-hunters' Chase at the main meeting of the year, the National Hunt Festival in March.

This meeting has a special excitement of its own for all jumping enthusiasts. Cheltenham demands every type of asset that a horse can possess–ability to race uphill and down, to jump uncompromising fences, and to have the courage to face a long uphill run from nearly half a mile out to a winning post which in heavy going seems not to be coming an inch nearer with each stride, as though in some nightmare.

There are few horses which have been great names in English steeplechasing who have not won at Cheltenham. The greatest of them all has been Arkle, the Irish-born gelding who won the 1964 Gold Cup from Mill House, and went on to win it again the next two years. Arkle became a legend. He had songs written about him, a cocktail named after him, a fan mail of his own, and when he damaged a bone in his foot in the King George VI Chase at Kempton Park on Boxing Day, 1967, it was as though the bottom had dropped out of the steeplechasing world. Hundreds of "get well" cards were posted to him from all over the world, people flocked to the racecourse stables at weekends to see the great horse with his damaged leg encased in plaster. The foot eventually healed enough for Arkle to return to steady exercise at Tom Dreaper's stables in Ireland, but his owner, the Duchess of Westminster, after some months of weighing the pros and cons, finally decided that she could not bear to risk Arkle suffering a much more serious injury if he was raced again. So the game lost a horse who was so far in advance of any of his contemporaries that it was necessary for the rules for handicap weights to be revised, and who earned affection not only for his ability but for the unashamed way in which he used to play to the gallery with bright eye, cocked ears and dancing feet as he made his way to the starting gate. He was finally put down in May 1970 after developing arthritis.

From out of Ireland have come so many fine steeplechasers that it is not surprising to find that nearly 75 per cent of all Grand National winners since 1900 are Irish-bred. Irish flat racing has become more sophisticated in the past 10 years and the increase in prize money has meant that racegoers have been able to see many more top-class horses from other countries competing, par-ticularly in the valuable Irish Sweeps Derby, but if there is one type of horse that appeals to the Irish, it is a real good steeplechaser.

There is no steeplechasing at The Curragh, head-quarters of Irish flat racing, but elsewhere the popularity of the sport is reflected in the fact that nearly every racecourse included chase and hurdle events with its flat races.

The fine record of success for Irish jumpers in England, and the big prizes that can be won now that sponsorship by commercial firms, and the prize money grants from the Horserace Betting Levy Board have put English National Hunt racing on a much higher plane than at any stage in its history, mean that Irish horses command hefty prices.

The appearance of an English owner or trainer looking for potential jumpers brings out the Irishman's natural talent for selling a horse well. The imbibing of "a jar or two" of the local beverage helps to lessen the shock when you are asked to look, possibly at dusk or in falling rain, at some gaunt gelding standing forlornly in a field, and learn that the owner puts a price of £6,000 on this piece of championship material, unraced to date–though he would be sorry to see him go, for wasn't his mother a half-sister to the dam of Mrs O'Callaghan's grand horse that won the amateurs' at Tralee the other day, and he had a mind to race the horse himself.

Buying expeditions to Ireland tend to stretch out much longer than anticipated because of that delightful national characteristic of never doing anything in a hurry, and never getting thirsty while doing it. A friend of ours once set out for Ireland on a Thursday, telling his wife he was going to look at a horse and would be back on the Monday. He actually returned on the Wednesday of the week following the one he had intended to return in, having paid £1,500 more for a horse than the limit he had set himself. He also had a hangover.

Irish jumping races take place on 27 different courses, with the Grand National run at Fairyhouse, the Galway Plate a 2 m. 5 f. chase and the Guinness Hurdle at Galway, and the Leopardstown Chase among the most important events. A course with all its own flavour is Punchestown, where they still race over natural banks. Until a few years ago, this type of racing could still be seen at point-to-points such as the Axe Vale in the West of England, where the horses generally jumped up onto the top of the banks, took one stride and then jumped off the other side, but now you have to go to Punchestown if you want to see it. Vast crowds flock to the meeting in December when the bank course is used (there are also conventional brush fence and hurdles courses) and bank racing has legendary stories all of its own. The course includes a stone wall, and a "double", a huge bank which Captain Machell, who won three Grand Nationals between 1873 and 1876 with Disturbance, Reugny and Regal, is supposed to have cleared with one leap when riding Kate Fisher.

We tend to think of international competition in racing as something that was invented since the Second World War, but, the records of the great European races show that our forefathers were far from averse to sending their horses abroad more than a hundred years ago, when shipping a horse from England or Ireland to France, or in the opposite direction, did not mean a couple of hours' flip in a plane, and motorised horse boxes in attendance at each end.

Irish steeplechasing in the 1880's was graced by Thomas Linde, who trained at Eyrefield Lodge on The Curragh, and who won the Liverpool Grand National with Empress and Woodbrook in 1880 and 1881. This superb horseman would never send a horse to the races unless it knew all about jumping the obstacles, and it is reported that on one occasion, for the entertainment of the Empress of Austria, who was on a hunting holiday in Ireland, a two-year-old was brought out by Linde and schooled twice round the steeplechase course, jumping impeccably.

Linde's ventures into international competition, apart from his Aintree forays, included the winning of two Grand Steeplechase de Paris, with two four-year-olds, Whisper Low and Too Good. The latter was the same horse that had delighted the Empress of Austria with his jumping skill at an age when most horses have scarcely learned to jump a molehill in the paddock. Nowadays four-year-olds are barred from running in the Grand Steeplechase, and the youngest entrants permitted are five.

French steeplechasing is a different kettle of fish again from Irish and English. Most of the courses are figure-of-eight and include a variety of types of fences. Speed, ability to gallop round turns, and versatility are what are required, and the heavily built staying steeplechaser from Ireland or England is often at a loss on French courses.

Stone walls crowned with turf, banks and single or double bars, sometimes with a brook on the landing side, a water jump with a small fence in front of it, open ditches, and bullfinches–fences of high, thin birch, which a horse has to jump through, not over–these are the sort of fences which make up a French steeplechase course such as that at Auteuil, close to the heart of Paris, where the Grand Steeplechase is run.

It was a horse from England, Miss Hungerford that won the first Grand Steeplechase in 1874, and it was one trained there, though bred in France, who put up the fantastic performance of winning the race 90 years later with a broken

There are more ways of falling than you could write a book about. The most spectacular mass fall was in the 1967 Grand National at Liverpool, when all the remaining runners fell, were brought down or stopped at the 23rd. fence leaving Foinavon, on the left with dark colours and light cross-belts, to head for the winning post, hopelessly pursued by remounted horses.

bridle. This was Mandarin, owned by Mme Peggy Hennessy of the famous cognac family, and ridden by Fred Winter, five times champion jumping jockey of England, who found, after jumping two fences that he was entirely without means of steering his horse round the tortuous course.

It may be unjust to say that, in the cut-throat competition that typifies flat racing, the other jockeys in the race would have left Winter to stew in his own juice, or would have deliberately given his a mount a nudge which would have sent him in the wrong direction at some stage during the four miles that had to be covered. But they did not, and at the first bend, when they had seen his plight–galloping at 30 miles an hour round a figure of eight course, one of them actually helped him round, by keeping his own horse half a length behind Mandarin and on the outside of the bend. After that Winter was on his own, and incredibly managed to keep Mandarin on the course, to jump all the fences, to take the lead between the last two fences, and to scrape past the winning post a few centimetres in front of the fast-finishing Lumino. This was truly one of the greatest performances in steeplechasing anywhere in the world.

French jumping courses are fairly typical of those to be found in most European countries, demanding a horse with speed and agility rather than stamina and ability to cope with huge impenetrable fences. The centre of the fine flat race courses at San Siro, Milan, and at Cologne are, for instance, occupied with a figure of eight jumping course on which races like the Gran Steeplechase di Milano are run. The winner of the Milano race has on a number of occasions been seen competing on French, Spanish and German courses.

With a character all its own is the Gran Pardubice Chase in Czechoslovakia. This is not a steeplechase in the same mould as those we see on most European courses, and approximates more to the old concept of point-to-point racing.

The obstacles are formidable–a huge water jump, a vast ditch at the top of a hill which if not met exactly right means that horse and rider disappear into a hole some eight foot deep. The pace at which the race is run is reflected in the fact that Grifel, Epigraff and Reljef, three Russian horses who were sent to Aintree to run without success in the Grand National, finished first, second and third in the Gran Pardubice, after the first two had both fallen and been remounted.

The jumping game is Australia is not as popular with the metropolitan crowds as flat racing. At Sydney there was jumping at Randwick until the early years of the Second World War, but now the steeplechase course, though its outline can still be seen, is used only for exercising horses.

At Caulfield, Melbourne, they run both the Australian Steeplechase and the Australian Hurdle, and there is jumping, too, on the sharp little track at Moonee Valley. Caulfield stages Australia's strongest metropolitan jumping programmes and during the antipodean winter, June and July, about half the card is made up of jumping races.

Australian steeplechase fences are made of brush and take nothing like as much jumping as those found on English courses, though Flemington, Melbourne, had some pretty fierce fences before the war, including a triangular pile of logs, a cement wall, and post and rails.

Outside the big cities in Australia, the best jumping is found at Onkaparinga, over 100 miles from Adelaide, and Warrnambool, about the same distance from Melbourne. Here jumping carnivals are held once a year and the large crowds that assemble see not only the racing but participate in barbecues, dances and parties. Both courses present the horses with much tougher fences than those found on the city tracks, and at Onkaparinga they have to negotiate a bitumen road in addition to the other hazards.

Steeplechasing in America is a sport which is struggling against the dislike of city racegoers for betting on races over the jumps. The standardised outline of the American flat track does not permit any variety in the jumping courses and as a spectacle steeplechasing suffers.

The richest jumping programmes were staged by the New York Racing Association at Aqueduct, Belmont Park and Saratoga with the Temple Gwathmey Steeplechase at $50,000.

American jumping enthusiasts received a severe set-back in 1972 when the N.Y.R.A. abolished jumping events at Aqueduct and Belmont Park, leaving Saratoga as the only track under their jurisdiction with steeplechase and hurdle events. There is no steeplechasing at all on the big Californian track and even prominent racing journalists in that part of the world have never heard of Neji, who set world record for a steeplechaser by winning $271,956 on eastern tracks.

Jump races are staged at Monmouth Park in New Jersey and Delaware Park, but for the nearest thing to an English steeplechase or point-to-point meeting you have to visit one of the hunt race meetings such as that at Middleburg, Virginia. Here spectators watch the horses being saddled and mounted in a tree-lined parade ring, and view the racing on undulating post-and-rail and brush courses from a terraced hillside which provides a natural grandstand.

Picnics from the back of a station wagon are popular and they too are a feature of the annual gathering for the Maryland Hunt Cup in the Worthington Valley not far from Baltimore. From a hillside, some 14,000 people watch the field for the day's only event gallop four miles over 22 unrelenting five-barred post-and-rail fences. In spite of the severity of the fences, the pace is almost as fast as that for the English Grand National, and at nearly 30 m.p.h., one touch of the top bar usually means disaster.

Three times a winner of this race was Jay Trump, who in between times crossed to England to win the Grand National and came within a touch of landing what might be described as the Triple Crown of international steeplechasing when he finished a close third in the Grand Steeplechase de Paris. Certainly he was one of jumping's most versatile horses and it was sad that his owner decided to retire him when he was only nine and still capable of great things.

More young owners are beginning to take an interest in American steeplechasing and it is hoped that the new $100,000 chase, the Colonial Cup at Camden, South Carolina, in November, 1970, will give encouragement to the sport. Part of the celebrations of the third centenary of the State of South Carolina, the race was designed to attract runners from a number of countries, and it created more interest than any other jumping race in America for many years.

Nine horses were flown over from Europe, including some of the best steeplechasers in England, Ireland and France, and the field included the Australian champion jumper Crisp. In the event, the American horses Top Bid, Shadow Brook and Jaunty took the first three places in front of the Irish-trained L'Escargot, but as in flat racing, international barriers are being broken down in steeplechasing, and the organisers intend to make the Colonial Cup an annual confrontation of horses from many countries.

Touchdown, Cheltenham

Grand National 1966—The winner, Anglo, on extreme right, misses the mishaps.

From top to bottom:
Hurdlers at Cheltenham
The big brook at Auteuil
Helping hands at Aintree

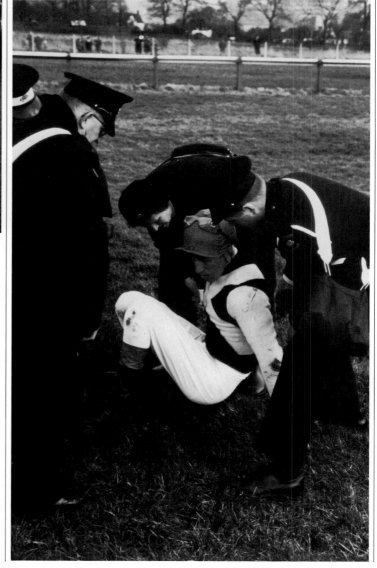

Twelve of the Best

What have been the best racehorses ever to set foot on a racecourse anywhere in the world? That kind of question, posed after dinner as the port goes round for the second time, or in the stable help canteen as the hip flasks are being pulled out after the day's work is over, can lead to reminiscence, argument on detail, friendly disagreement, or full-blooded table pounding, because one of the most difficult things in the world of racing is to compare one generation of racehorses with another, or to set a standard for horses performing in different parts of the world.

It is with some trepidation, therefore, that the author embarks on the project of looking at the records of the twelve best racehorses that, in his opinion, have run during the past 100 years. No one is going to agree on the short list–but what a marvellous subject upon which to disagree. As the winter winds shake the shutters, throw another log on the fire and remember the time when you saw this horse or that break the track record, giving lumps of weight to his nearest rival! "Could have fallen down at the furlong pole, got up again and still won."

Perhaps, but the nearest that any horse has ever come to doing that was probably the filly Sun Chariot, who won England's Triple Crown for fillies, the 1,000 Guineas, Oaks and St. Leger, for King George VI in 1942. Before the Oaks, Sun Chariot had developed regrettable tendencies at the start of a gallop, and on one occasion when the King visited the stables of her trainer, Fred Darling, at Beckhampton in Wiltshire, she carried champion jockey Gordon Richards into a ploughed field before the start of a gallop and went down on her knees, roaring like a bull, before consenting to work.

For the Oaks, Sun Chariot was in an equally bad mood and she ruined three starts before the field eventually got on their way. But when the barrier went up, she did not go with the other runners. She darted off to the left, and the field had covered nearly a furlong before Gordon Richards had induced Sun Chariot to cover 50 yards.

Let Gordon Richards tell the story himself: "I remember thinking how very disappointed the King must be, looking through his glasses from the other end of the course. After we had gone nearly a mile, Sun Chariot reached the rest of the field. Then she began to thread her way through them. Suddenly I began to have hope again. Three furlongs from home she was going so well that I

Ribot
Kincsem
Phar Lap

decided to let her canter on without touching her. She went straight on and won nicely by a length. It was one of the most amazing performances I have ever known."

Rightly or wrongly, Sun Chariot does not get a place in our list of the Top Twelve. It was a substandard wartime field that she cut through and her record afterwards at stud was not brilliant, though she did produce Landau, who became a successful stallion in Australia.

So what are the standards by which one judges the best horses of the past century? As two geldings are in the list, it is obviously not based on ability to transfer brilliance to succeeding generations. What is interesting is that more than half the horses in the list has been involved in international competition. This was not set as one of the criteria when this personal list was drawn up, but it became evident when the dozen were arrived at that participation in international competition, with success, was evident in many cases.

Here is the list:

RIBOT (1952)
KINCSEM (1874)
PHAR LAP (1926)
HYPERION (1930)
MAN O'WAR (1917)
KELSO (1951)
TANTIEME (1947)
NEARCO (1936)
THE TETRARCH (1911)
SCEPTRE (1899)
ST SIMON (1881)
ORMONDE (1883)

Two fillies, two geldings, eight colts, from a wide area. Who can say if I am right or wrong, but, with one exception, the temptation to give the twelve any order of preference has been avoided. That would be too presumptious, but I do express an opinion that Ribot is the best of the lot.

They said that Ribot was not a good looking horse when he was racing. He was not a bad looking one. He was unbeaten in 16 races, he raced in Italy, France and England, and since he went to stud there has scarcely been a season when he has not been responsible for a horse of the highest quality running in Europe of America.

He was bred in Italy by that genius of the thoroughbred industry, Federico Tesio, who died before seeing in action the result of the mating he planned for his Italian Derby winner Tenerani, and the mare Romanella, who had won one of Italy's top two-year-old races, the Criterium Nazionale. He did, however, say of Ribot, who was the despised one of the 1952 crop of foals at the Dormello Stud, "This little one will be somebody one day." How right he was.

Hyperion
Man O'War
The Tetrarch

Tantieme
Nearco
Kelso

201

Sceptre
St. Simon
Ormonde

Ribot's first seven victories were in Italy, at Milan and Pisa, but Dormello has never been afraid to test its best horses against international opposition, and in October, 1955, Ribot was sent to Paris to contest the Prix de l'Arc de Triomphe. Ribot won easily from a field that included Zarathustra, winner of the 1954 Irish Derby, and Rapace, winner of the 1955 French Derby. In addition the field included eight horses who had been placed in or had won the classic races of England, Ireland and France during the past two seasons.

The following season, Ribot resumed his winning run with four victories on that stern galloping course at San Siro, Milan, before going to Ascot for the King George VI and Queen Elizabeth Stakes. This race, in its sixth year, had established itself as one of the premier international prizes. It has to be admitted that the field that opposed Ribot was not impressive, but for the first time in his life the Italian colt had to contend with going that was dead. For a moment when he turned into the straight in fourth place, it looked as though the ground might bog him down, but like a true champion, he accelerated and won by five lengths from the Queen's horse High Veldt.

Ribot went home to Italy and collected a small race at San Siro before returning to Paris for his second Prix de l'Arc de Triomphe. He won this in breathtaking style. That great international expert on racing and breeding, the late Captain Kasimir Bobinski, summed up the race when he wrote "Those who were lucky enough to see the terrific burst of speed produced by Ribot in the last stage of his race will never forget it. Only a real champion could show such brilliant acceleration at the end of a race run at such a strong pace. I cannot help thinking that his jockey, Camici, rode this race for the public. He must have been determined to do something to silence the critics and move the sceptics. This he did without needing to pick up his whip; a glorious finale to a magnificent horse's career."

Ribot retired to stud, first in England at Lord Derby's stud, then in Italy at the Razza Dormello-Olgiata where he was bred, and finally in America, at the Darby Dan Farm, Lexington, Kentucky. It was intended that he should return to Italy after a five year stay in America, but by this time he had become so difficult to handle that it was decided that the plane journey back to Italy would be unsafe. He has sired a succession of champions, including Molvedo, who, like him, won the Prix de l'Arc de Triomphe, Tom Rolfe, the best American three-year-old of 1962, Ribocco, winner of the St. Leger and the Irish Sweeps Derby, and America's Horse of the Year, Arts and Letters.

Fully exposed to the best opposition that half a

dozen countries could offer, Ribot beat them all, and passed on his talent to succeeding generations. What more can you ask of a horse?

On the outskirts of Newmarket stands a bronze statue by John Skeaping of one of the smallest thoroughbreds to go into training, one of the gamest, and one that has had more influence on breeding around the world than any other horse of recent generations. This is Hyperion, who would have been hard put to it to match strides with Ribot, but whose name is known in every country where racing takes place.

Hyperion was so small when he was foaled at the Earl of Derby's Woodland Stud near Newmarket that he was not sent into training with the other yearlings in 1931. But Lord Derby's private trainer, the Honourable George Lambton, was so impressed with his action and with his character that he decided to let him take his chance.

Hyperion never grew to more than 15.1½ hands, but he won nine of his thirteen races, was unbeaten as a three-year-old, and was successful in the Epsom Derby and the St. Leger.

He was all his life a great character. John Hislop, journalist and breeder, recalls that Hyperion was extremely fond of his trainer. When he saw George Lambton (who had been seriously ill) in a wheel chair before the Ascot Gold Cup, he refused to leave him for some time. When he was in training he would sometimes stop and stand still for half an hour or more, gazing into the distance, but Lambton would never allow him to be touched, just waiting until he wanted to move on.

Hyperion sired the winners of ten English classics and horses such as Pensive, successful in the 1941 Kentucky Derby, and Aureole who carried Queen Elizabeth II's colours to victory in the King George VI and Queen Elizabeth Stakes at Ascot in 1950. He sired the unpredictable but brilliant Sun Chariot, and the list of the best horses produced by Hyperion mares covers every major racing country in the world, and many others besides.

Visitors to Newmarket should never miss seeing the statue of Hyperion, about threequarters of a mile out of town on the Snailwell Road and close to the paddock where the little horse who has had such an enormous influence on world breeding was foaled.

Hyperion is the great grand-sire of a horse who probably earned more affection from the American racing public than any other racehorse within living memory, but who will never hand on any of his own ability, for the simple reason that he is a gelding.

Kelso, by Your Host, by Alibhai, by Hyperion, was the horse who captured the public's imagination in the mid 1960's in a manner unequalled by any other, and who earned himself the title of American Horse of the Year for five consecutive years. His sire, Your Host, was a cripple but Kelso himself galloped his way into the headlines of not only America but the world, with his 39 victories in 63 starts, and his world record total of earnings of $1,977,986.

Kelly, as he was affectionately known by his owner, Mrs Richard C. duPont, put up one of his greatest performances when he won the Washington D.C. International in 1964 in the world record for a 1½ m. turf course of 2m. 23 4/5ths seconds.

Kelso was one of those horses who ran and ran and ran, and gave his utmost every time. His performance in the Washington D.C. International was electrifying, and whenever he ran there was a substantial increase in attendance. He is one of the few horses ever to have had a book entirely devoted to himself, and probably the only one to have had souvenir sugar especially wrapped with his name on the outside. In one drawer of my desk there are half a dozen cubes of sugar wrapped in the grey and yellow colours of Mrs duPont's stable and bearing the words "Bohemia Stable…Kelso and his friends".

Stars like Kelso happen to racing only once in a while. They stand above the horses who year by year attract the attention and loyalty of the regular racing fan, and they bring into the sport many others who stood on the perimeter. Of such material was Arkle in Irish and English steeplechasing, Kelso in American flat racing, Phar Lap in Australia, and Man o'War, beaten only once in 21 races in the U.S.A.

Breeding purists may look aghast at the inclusion in this chapter of such horses as Kelso and Phar Lap, who were never capable of handing on their brilliance to succeeding generations, but you cannot ignore Phar Lap. He, like Kelso, had a book written about him, and his racing record completely justifies that event.

Phar Lap's story came to an end when he died in Mexico in 1931 after coasting home in a minor race in which he had covered probably half a furlong more than any of the other runners because his rider had been warned that attempts would be made to interfere with the horse during the race.

It is probably an exaggeration to say that something approaching a state of war existed between Australia and America after Phar Lap had died, but the other day an Australian secretary who was not even thought of when it all happened remarked when discussing Phar Lap, "That was terrible, what the Americans did to him."

Phar Lap was a horse who won 37 races, at distances from six furlongs to two miles, who won the A.J.C. Derby in Sydney and the Victoria Racing Club Derby in Melbourne in identical world record times of 2 m. 31 1/2 secs. (this has since been beaten), who carried 9st. 12 lb. to an effortless victory in the Melbourne Cup as a four-year-old, and finished third the next year under the crushing burden of 10st. 10lb.

A horse of kindly temperament, he became a racing machine once on the course. He could win at two miles and a few outings later match the speed of seven furlongs horses.

He cantered home in his one race at Caliente just over the Mexican border and looked all set for a tour of American tracks when he was found dead in his box. An autopsy showed suggestions of poisoning by arsenic, but the mystery has never been cleared up. Dr Stewart Mackay, author of a book called "Staying Power on the Racehorse", which was actually a paeon of praise for Phar Lap, took part in the autopsy, reported that the great horse's heart weighed 14 1/2 lb., compared to the 10lb. of another racehorse examined.

Thousands of column inches have been devoted to Phar Lap in Australian newspapers and magazines. He is still a household word, and the yardstick against which good Australian horses will be measured for many years to come.

Man o'War? Well he went to the starting gate 21 times, and he won 20 times. The only horse who ever beat him was called appropriately enough Upset, and the American Racing Manual, that superb guide to racing in both America and other parts of the world, still publishes every year the chart of that race over six furlongs at Saratoga, in August, 1919.

During his career, Man o'War won nearly $250,000, which was a lot of money in those days, was successful in the Preakness Stakes and the Belmont Stakes, the last two legs of the American triple crown, and broke five track records at Belmont Park and Aqueduct.

He was a proud horse of great character and his influence is felt throughout the world of breeding today. His sons Clyde van Dusen and War Admiral won the Kentucky Derby in 1929 and 1937 respectively (War Admiral also won the Preakness and the Belmont Stakes and is one of only eight American Triple Crown winners) and his daughter Singing Grass produced Never Say Die, champion English stallion in 1962. There are other American horses for whom it will be argued that they are entitled to a place in this list, including such as Nashua, Swaps, Seabiscuit and Count Fleet, Buckpasser, Damascus, Bold Ruler, Dr. Fager, Citation and Native Dancer but if it comes to sheer ability on the track and stud performance, we settle for Man o'War. On the count of stud performance, Kelso gets a zero, but as a racehorse he was one of the most exciting things we have seen in action.

In 1898 John Porter, trainer of Kingsclere, wrote, "I have readily expressed the opinion that Ormonde was the greatest horse I have ever known. There are some of my contemporaries who think that St. Simon was his superior… we must agree to differ."

The facts are that Ormonde went through his racing life unbeaten. He ran sixteen times and his sixteen victories included England's Triple Crown, the 2,000 Guineas, the Derby and the St. Leger. After Ormonde had won the Derby by a length and a half from The Bard, who was unbeaten in 16 races as a two-year-old, his trainer said: "I was now absolutely certain that in Ormonde I had the best horse that had ever been under my care. Look at the horses Ormonde defeated! He was a giant among giants."

But before he ran in the St. Leger, Ormonde started making a whistling noise when he galloped, and during the winter of 1886–87 an electric sponge was applied every day to the paralysed nerve in his throat which had resulted in him making a noise". The effect of the treatment seems to have been negligible, for one morning early in his four-year-old season, his trainer could hear him breathing in thick fog on the gallops when he was nearly half a mile away.

But if he made a noise, it had no effect on his galloping abilities. He went on winning, and his last three races give additional insight to his brilliance. He won the Rous Memorial Stakes over a mile on the first day of the Royal Ascot meeting in June, and the Hardwicke Stakes over a mile and a half on the second day, beating Minting who had been second to him in the 2,000 Guineas the year before. As the horses went to the post, Minting's trainer, Matt Dawson, told John Porter, "You'll be beaten today, John. No horse with Ormonde's infirmity can hope to beat Minting." In the race, Ormonde was badly hampered by the three-year-old Phil, whose jockey George Barrett thought he should have been riding the great horse and was furious that Tom Cannon had been engaged. Ormonde came back with one leg badly grazed, but he still beat Minting a neck.

And finally he won the Imperial Gold Cup at Newmarket over six furlongs, giving six pounds and a two lengths beating to a sprinter called Whitefriar. To come back from the mile and a half of the Hardwicke Stakes to six furlongs and win comfortably was the performance of a brilliant horse.

His owner, the Duke of Westminster, sold Ormonde to the Argentine as a stallion because he thought that roaring was an hereditary complaint and he did not want to be accused of spreading it through the many high-class mares which would obviously be sent to him. After three seasons in

South America he was bought by a wealthy Californian breeder, Mr William Macdonough, for £30,000 which in 1883 was big money, and he was shipped to Mr Haggin's Rancho del Paso. But by the time he reached California, Ormonde was impotent and he did not sire a single foal. He was chloroformed to death in May, 1904 and buried at Menlo Park, to be exhumed a few months later so that his skeleton could be returned to the Natural History Museum in London. A sad end to a great horse.

There are two mares in the list, Kincsem and Sceptre. Kincsem had a record which ranged over 54 races and five different countries. She was never beaten, and if she had lived in the age of the aeroplane, instead of having to travel by horse-drawn van, by boat and by train, one wonders what she would have achieved.

One of the few individual racehorses commemorated on a postage stamp, Kincsem was foaled in 1874 and visited Germany, France, Austria and England, as well as winning many races in her native Hungary. She won the Grosser Preis von Baden three times, the Austrian Derby, the Grand Prix de Deauville, and the Goodwood Cup, and collected the Hungarian 2,000 Guineas, the Oaks and the St. Leger.

It can be argued that the opposition was not always formidable but she just kept on winning–54 times. She had only three sons and two daughters, and between them they landed 41 European classic races and some 30 cups.

Sceptre was a filly who reached incredible heights in spite of being owned by an ex-bookmaker turned gambler, Bob Sievier, who treated her as a machine rather than a racehorse.

Sievier made a small fortune in Australia as a bookmaker and returned to England in 1900, some time before the Melbourne Cup winner of 1899, The Grafter, arrived for an English campaign. Sievier judged The Grafter as a good bet in Epsom's big spring handicap, the City and Suburban, went to see the horse in his pre-race work, and backed him to win £35,000. The Grafter won easily, and Sievier went from strength to strength that year, playing up his winnings.

In the Autumn of 1900 he paid 10,000 guineas for a filly at the dispersal sale of the Duke of Westminster's Eaton Stud, where Ormonde was bred, and named her Sceptre. The filly won a couple of races as a two-year-old, but it was as a three-year-old that she showed her true ability.

Sceptre was engaged in all five classic races, and normally one would not expect her to be seen on a racecourse until two or three weeks before the first of them, the 2,000 Guineas. But Bob Sievier had had a disastrous winter's gambling at Monte Carlo, and gave orders for her to be prepared for the Lincolnshire Handicap, the first big handicap of the season. She was caught on the post and beaten a head by the French horse St. Maclou, which cost Sievier £30,000. He sacked his trainer Charles Martin and took charge of Sceptre himself.

Sceptre won the 2,000 Guineas in a canter and in record time, and two days later beat her contemporary fillies in the 1,000 Guineas after having a twisted plate wrenched off just before the start. Ten days before the Derby she went lame, but Sievier, who had backed her to win £30,000, ran her and saw her finish fourth. Two days later she was saddled again and won the Oaks in a canter.

Sievier slipped Sceptre over to Paris to run in the Grand Prix. In those days foreign visitors could expect rough treatment from the French jockeys and Sceptre's jockey kept well clear of the rest of the field. The filly covered a great deal more ground than anything else, and finished fourth. Back in England a few days later she was beaten in the Coronation Stakes at Ascot, and then won the St. James's Palace Stakes the very next day. At Goodwood she was beaten in one race, pulled out again two days later and won the Nassau Stakes. At Doncaster, she beat the colts in the St. Leger, was asked to run again in the Park Hill Stakes two days later, and was beaten.

Sievier, now heavily in debt in spite of Sceptre's wins, had one last gamble on her in the Lincolnshire Handicap the following March, but she ran unplaced. She was sold to Mr William Bass for 25,000 guineas and retired to stud. From her have descended the sires and dams of many good horses, but one wonders just how much better her own record would have been if she had been in more sympathetic hands.

Undoubtedly one of the greatest racehorses and sires that lived was Sceptre's grandsire, St. Simon, who never ran in the classics because his owner Prince Batthyany died when the colt was a two-year-old, nullifying all his engagements under the Jockey Club rules of those days.

Those who saw St Simon race said that he gave a tremendous impression of pent-up energy, and moved as if made of elastic. Bought by the Duke of Portland at the dispersal of Batthyany's bloodstock, he ran in nine races and was unbeaten. In his fourth race, the Prince of Wales's Nursery at Doncaster, he carried top weight of nine stone and, conceding between 27 lb. and 44 lb. to his twenty opponents, cantered in eight lengths clear of the nearest horse. In a match against a horse called Duke of Richmond, who was considered one of the best two-year-olds in the country, St. Simon was fifty yards ahead after going only a quarter of a mile, until his rider, the great Fred

Archer, eased him to coast home by threequarters of a length.

His most important win was in the Ascot Gold Cup. Archer could not get down to the necessary weight, and the ride went to George Wood. The jockey managed to settle him, but when he gave St. Simon a little rein in the straight, the horse bounded forward and sprinted home 20 lengths ahead of Tristan, who had won the Gold Cup the previous year, and who showed there was nothing wrong with the form by coming out the day after his defeat by St. Simon to win the Hardwicke Stakes.

St. Simon's trainer, Matt Dawson, said that the great horse was as fast over a furlong as he was over three miles. He left an indellible mark on the breed, and there is no country in the world where descendants of St. Simon have not gained fame and fortune. He sired the winners of 571 races, and ten of his sons and daughters won seventeen English classic races. In 1900 all five of the classics went to his offspring, Diamond Jubilee, Winifreda and La Roche.

So far in this list of great horses there has been no mention of one from France, the country which is now staging the best racing in Europe, and probably the world. The Prix de l'Arc de Triomphe, which year after year sets a higher standard of competition than any other mile and a half race, has set the seal on the racing career of many horses to whom the term "brilliant" could be applied–such as Ribot, Vaguely Noble, Exbury and Sea Bird. The last three, all trained in France, showed pulverising speed in the straight at Longchamp to transform their races, against opponents of the highest class, in such a way that those who saw them perform had little doubt that they were in the presence of real champions.

And what of Pharis, who was racing in France when the threat of war clouded everything, but who is remembered by those who saw him perform as one of the best that France has ever produced. Owned and bred by M. Marcel Boussac, Pharis ran only three times and won every race–a mile and a half event at Longchamp, the Prix du Jockey Club (French Derby) at Chantilly and the Grand Prix de Paris at Longchamp. In the last two races, he made up an incredible amount of ground in the straight, after being hopelessly placed, to win comfortably.

He was shipped to England with the objective of taking on the English Derby winner, Blue Peter, in the St. Leger, but a few days before the race war broke out and the Doncaster meeting never took place. Some more evidence would have helped one to decide if Pharis should have been included in this arguable list of great horses, and we have selected instead Tantieme, twice winner of the Prix de l'Arc de Triomphe, in 1950 and 1951.

Tantieme was the best of a first-class crop, though he was unluckily defeated in the French Derby. He raced from two years to four, he won his only two races as a two-year-old, including the Grand Criterium, and at three he took seven races, including the French 2,000 Guineas (Poule d'Essai des Poulains) and the Queen Elizabeth Stakes at Ascot before winning the Prix de l'Arc de Triomphe for the first time. In the Queen Elizabeth Stakes, his jockey Roger Poincelet waited on him and he got up only in the last strides to win by a head from another French horse, Coronation V, who had won the previous year's Prix de l'Arc de Triomphe.

The following year Tantieme won four races in France including his second Arc de Triomphe, and crossed to England twice. He was not a good traveller, but he landed the Coronation Cup at Epsom comfortably, though he had worked himself into a lather before the race. For his next visit to England, it was decided to fly him over on the very morning of the race, the King George VI and Queen Elizabeth Stakes. He appeared cool and collected in the paddock, but in the race he gave away lengths by running wide turning into the straight and was beaten into third place by Supreme Court. He was a big success at stud, and his progeny included Match, winner of the Washington D. C. International, and Reliance, who won the French Derby, Grand Prix de Paris and French St. Leger (Prix Royal Oak).

At the December Sales in 1915, when bloodstock prices were rock bottom as the First World War entered its second grim year, Italy's brilliant breeder Signor Federico Tesio bought for 75 guineas an insignificant mare of American ancestry called Catnip, who proved one of the biggest bargains in the history of racing. Catnip produced Nogara, who bred six winners, including Nearco, unbeaten in 14 races.

Nearco had seven races as a two-year-old, and soon established a reputation that frightened away most of the opposition when ever he was due to run. As a three-year-old he started off by winning at seven furlongs, and his six victories included the Italian 2,000 Guineas, the Italian Derby, which he won by a distance, and the Gran Premio di Milano.

Tesio's belief in testing his good horses against the best in Europe once they had established their reputation at home meant that six days after the Gran Premio, Nearco appeared in Paris, after an arduous train journey from Milan, to take on Bois Roussel and Cillas, winners of the English and French Derbys, in the Grand Prix de Paris. Also in the field were the winners of the French 1,000

Guineas (Poule d'Essai des Pouliches) and the French Oaks (Prix de Diane). Always going well, Nearco took the lead entering the Longchamp straight and ran on strongly to win impressively.

A few days after the race, Tesio sold Nearco to an English bookmaker, Mr Martin Benson. The price was £60,000, then a record, and Nearco went immediately to the Beech House Stud on the outskirts of Newmarket. His influence on the breed has been remarkable. He was for 15 years in the top ten sires in England and champion sire twice. He sired the winners of two English Derbys two Oaks, a St. Leger and a 2,000 Guineas and countless other high-class winners, while his daughters have bred many more. His son Nasrullah, temperamental but brilliant, has been one of the most influential sires in American breeding, and got among many others, Nashua, who won $1,288,565; and Bold Ruler, like himself a champion sire.

And finally "The Rocking Horse" or "The Spotted Wonder"–the grey colt called The Tetrarch, who raced only as a two-year-old but who convinced his brilliant trainer Atty Persse and all who saw him that this was a horse of exceptional ability. He won all seven of his races, including the National Breeders Produce Stakes at Sandown Park, which he landed by only a neck. As visibility was bad, those in the stands were unaware that The Tetrarch, who owed his nicknames to his grey coat covered with whitish blotches, had almost collided with the tapes at the start and was actually back-pedalling when they rose. He then leapt forward and struck the hind quarters of another runner and by the time his jockey, the great Steve Donoghue, had him settled, he had given away many lengths to the leaders.

Sadly, The Tetrarch did not stand training as a three-year-old, and further evidence of his brilliance, apart from the manner in which he won on the course, must be drawn from his performances in a series of trial gallops in his two-year-old days. In April, when a two-year-old is little more than adolescent and should receive 47 lb. from an aged horse (one over six years old), he was asked to give 10 lb. to one called Captain Symons, who won a good race at Chester a few weeks later. He beat Captain Symons effortlessly.

Again, before he won the Coventry Stakes at Ascot by ten lengths, The Tetrarch was tried against older horses, among them Noromac, who won a good sprint at Sandown Park with 8 st. 10 lb. shortly afterwards. He gave Noromac 10 lb., and beat him 10 lengths.

It was a tragedy that this spectacular colt, with his huge stride, was unable to run the following year. From time to time, grey descendants of his, bearing something resembling the striking splotches he wore, appear on the racecourse, but none has shown the electrifying speed that he demonstrated in gallops and in contest.

You may disagree with the selection of the twelve best horses of the past hundred years. But all of them had the magnetism of great stars and the ability to draw thousands of people to the tracks. Those who promote racing would be happy if just one such star would come their way every year.

An Eye on the Criminal

It is a sad fact that any human enterprise which involves the movement of large sums of money from one place to another or from one person to another will attract the attention of those who would change the destination of that money for their own benefit. Banks, airlines and jewel merchants, are well aware of the facts of life and take the necessary precautions, though such is the ingenuity of man, not always with complete success. The racing organisations of many countries in recent years, too, have had to keep abreast with the workings of the criminal mind.

Enormous amounts of money are at stake in racing and it is inevitable that from time to time the sport should attract the attention of criminals. Racing is, in the major countries where the sport is policed with increasing vigilance, a good deal straighter than newspaper headlines and the public might suggest. But however much money the racing authorities may spend on security measures, there will always be a tendency for the men in the street or the bettor in the grandstand to think that there are dark reasons for the horse that he has backed not winning a race, or for the success of another that he considered to have no chance.

A crime that is particularly reprehensible for a trainer to commit is to run two horses in the same race, and to win with the one least fancied in the betting. I recall that eminent and respected Yorkshire trainer the late Captain Charles Elsey showing me a letter he had received, unsigned and including the most dreadful language and imputations against the Captain's character, the day after he had had a horse win at 100 to 6, while his second runner which started at 5 to 2 had been unplaced.

The Captain usually had a cheerful twinkle in his eye and managed to get amusement out of most situations, but he was clearly distressed by this letter. "The only reason I had two runners in the one race was that both the owners live near the meeting and both of them wanted to win this particular race" he said. "I had never tried the two horses together at home and hadn't the foggiest idea which was the better at the weights. I didn't have a bet on the race, but this fellow thinks I am an out-and-out rogue."

Rogues there have always been in the history of racing, and always will be, though the standard of security in many countries is so greatly improved that it has become increasingly difficult for them to pervert the course of racing. It is difficult, for instance, to imagine the scandal of the English Derby of 1844 being repeated since the introduction of lip tattoo numbers to aid the identification of horses in America, and in Europe of the passports listing horses' identity marks.

This Derby was won by a horse called Running Rein, who was eventually proved to have been not a three-year-old of that name, but a four-year-old called Maccabaeus. Both horses were in the ownership of a gambler, Mr Goodman Levy, and the change in identity took place when the real Running Rein was a two-year-old. The appearance of Maccabaeus in a two-year-old race at Newmarket in the name of Running Rein, which he won after being backed from 10 to 1 to 3 to 1, prompted one journalist to remark that he looked "as well furnished as many of our bona fide three-year-olds", but the official enquiry which followed came to a halt when a stable hand who was present when the real Running Rein was foaled, identified the horse who had won the Newmarket pace as the genuine article–no doubt under the influence of a handsome present from Mr Levy.

But Lord George Bentinck, member of the Jockey Club and one of the watchdogs of the Turf, was dissatisfied and during the winter he collected a large amount of evidence in case Running Rein should appear for the 2,000 Guineas in the Spring. Mr Levy decided, however, to wait for the Derby. Five days before that race Bentinck and two others presented a petition to the Stewards of the Epsom meeting asking them to enquire into the identity of Running Rein, and particularly to have the horse's teeth examined by a veterinary surgeon so that his age could be determined. The Stewards took the amazing decision that, without any examination, the horse would be permitted to run, but in the event of his winning, the stakes would be withheld until an enquiry had been conducted.

Running Rein duly won what appears to have been one of the roughest Derbies in history, and Colonel Peel, whose Orlando was second, lodged a claim for the stakes. Payment of very large sums in bets and sweepstakes were withheld and the Jockey Club took no action until a legal case had been settled between Colonel Peel and Mr A. Wood, a corn merchant at Epsom in whose name Running Rein appeared and who, it has been generously suggested, was an innocent dupe of Mr Levy's unaware of the true age of the animal.

The judge, Baron Anderson, repeatedly demanded that Running Rein should be produced, but obviously the horse's connections could not risk this, and eventually they withdrew from the case, leaving Lord George Bentinck's suspicions and his police work vindicated. Mr Goodman Levy and his friends, who had expected to win something in the region of £50,000, left the country in a hurry.

What underlines the dreadful state of affairs on the turf at this time was the fact that Running Rein was not the only horse in the 1844 Derby who was not a three-year-old. It happened that during the race, Running Rein collided with Leander, owned by two German brothers called Lichtwald. Leander fell with a broken leg. There had been suspicions that this horse was senior to the others with whom he was competing, and a post-mortem examination after he had been destroyed revealed that he was a year too old to qualify for the Derby. Roger Mortimer records in his history of the Derby that the Lichtwald brothers were furious at being barred from the English turf for life, and denounced the English as a race of liars. One of the brothers indignantly added that Leander had not been four at all, but six.

In the 19th century backing a horse ante-post, weeks or months before the event, was an even more hazardous operation than it is today. In addition to the usual problems of illness and lameness, horses were subject to vicious attacks from those with connections with the bookmaking fraternity who had an interest in preventing them arriving at the starting gate.

Typical was the case of Wild Dayrell, who won one race as a two-year-old in 1854, beat some older horses to whom he was giving a lot of weight in a gallop the following June, and was heavily backed for the Derby, only the second race of his career. In spite of the weight of money, his price in the market did not shorten, which was suspicious. Then his owner was offered £5,000 not to run the colt, which he refused, and the trainer was advised that the van which would take Wild Dayrell to Epsom would be interfered with. As an experiment, a bullock was put in the van, and as soon as it was moved, the wheels collapsed, the van toppled over, and one of the bullock's legs was broken. Wild Dayrell eventually reached Epsom in one piece and won the big race comfortably, but his owner declared that he never wanted to own another Derby horse.

Security in England has improved enormously since those days, and indeed since 1961, when Sir Victor Sassoon's horse Pinturischio was "got at" before the Derby. He was prevented from running in the Dante Stakes, one of the important Derby trial races at York, having been found with a high temperature, and was again found in a sorry condition a week before the Derby. Tests taken showed that he had been poisoned, and he never ran again.

To allege that the bookmaking profession is entirely responsible for events such as these would be irresponsible, but they do provide the facilities for others to take advantage of the crime, and there is direct evidence that they themselves are not averse to making use of the knowledge of the information that a certain horse has been interfered with. The author recalls a well known Midlands bookmaker complaining bitterly to him about "these fellows" who came to him with information that so-and-so had been got at and that he could lay the horse to as much as they liked. "I've laid them all down the book," said the bookmaker, "and then seen them trot home an easy winner. They'd never been got at, and the man who gave me the info was just hoping they would get beat anyway." His righteous indignation at being misinformed would have been more convincing if he had taken steps to advise the Jockey Club's security force the moment he was advised of what was supposed to be afoot.

There are some frauds in racing which have been so ingenious and so smoothly carried out that at a distance of years, and as one whose pocket was not hurt by what occurred, the inclination is to stand back and say, "Well, they deserved to win." Into this category must come the classic case of Trodmore races, in 1880. This was in the days when communications were not as fast as they are today, and when betting shops abounded illegally in London, particularly in the Fleet Street area.

Shortly before the Easter Bank Holiday, the editor of Bell's Life in London, a paper which was later amalgamated into the Sporting Life, received a letter from a gentleman who described himself as the secretary of Trodmore races, asking him to publish the Easter Monday programme in his paper. The Editor agreed, the list of runners duly arrived and appeared in the paper. It had been arranged that the secretary would also send in the results of the meeting for publication, a service which he offered as the editor was no doubt short of staff on this particularly busy day for racing.

In the evening the results arrived by telegram, were set in type and appeared in the paper the next day. It was only after a number of betting shop proprietors had paid out several thousand pounds to people who had had an amazing run of luck in backing winners at Trodmore that they began asking where the hell it was. By the time that everyone had discovered that it never existed, it was far too late to do anything about it.

An ingenious fraud of much later date that went wrong largely because of greed on the part of some of the gang of bookmakers involved was that concerning the horse Francasal who won a selling race for two-year-olds at Bath in July 1953. The animal that passed the winning post first was in fact later proved to have been a three-year-old named Santa Amarro, who had been shipped from France and had changed his identity after his arrival in England.

The mere fact of running a three-year-old which had won two races in France in a two-year-old seller at a minor meeting in England should have been enough to guarantee a good win from the bookmakers around the country with whom the horse was backed, but one element of the gang tried to gild the lily by cutting the telephone wires leading to Bath racecourse. This ensured that bookmakers who found themselves with heavy liabilities over the alleged Francasal would have no opportunity of sending money back to the course via the Exchange Telegraph and the "blower" telephone services which at that time offered this facility, thus forcing the course bookmakers to shorten the price.

Unluckily for them, a member of the gang was seen climbing a telegraph pole and cutting phone wires near the course just before the race. The racecourse was out of touch with the rest of the country for some time, but the combination of this circumstance and the enormous amount of money which was invested on Francasal, succeeded in alerting the racing world to what was happening The gang involved served sentences in prison of up to two years, and one of them, a Welsh bookmaker named Gomer Charles, later came to a bad end when he was shot dead at his front door by two men who were after the large sums of money which he was believed to keep in his bungalow.

The manipulation of odds on the course at small meetings in England, where the racecourse market is weak, coincidental with the backing of horses with bookmakers away from the course is a strategy which is easier today than ever before because the Government has, by its betting taxes, reduced the course betting market to a woefully weak state.

A classic case of manipulation some years ago was that involving a horse called C.D.B. at the Bank Holiday meeting at Huntingdon in May 1953. C.D.B. had won a race at Hurst Park in March that year, beating a number of useful horses, and run a good fourth in his next race. In the opinion of many he had an excellent chance in moderate company at Huntingdon. Another horse, with the unflattering name of The Moke, was made favourite, but C.D.B. could be backed at about 7 to 4. However, two or three of the bookmakers from whom the sporting newspaper reporter responsible for taking the starting prices was noting the odds, combined to make sure that the reporter was well aware that C.D.B. was on offer at 25 to 1 when the race started. And that was the price that was wired to newspapers and betting offices all over the country after racing.

It was then that the fireworks started, for a number of the leading bookmaking firms discovered that they had enormous commitments over C.D.B. For a while some of them refused to pay out, but they had no real case, as the return of 25 to 1 was official, though if the money invested all over the country had got back to the course, the price would have been something like three to one on.

(It should be pointed out that the starting price reporter was not one of those who conscientiously carry out this task on British racecourses day in and day out without fear of favour, but was one pressed into service on a day when there are usually no fewer than 16 holiday race meetings.)

I travelled back from Yarmouth races one day with one of the gang involved in this fraud, who said that the pay-out took place in a small room above the bar of a well known public house just off Fleet Street. It appears that guns and knives were taken along as trouble among those concerned was expected, but the pay-out went off without anyone getting his head blown off. The sum involved was over £200,000.

English racing towards the end of the 19th century was considerably less of a jungle than it was at the time that the Running Rein scandal was the talk of the turf, but it was not until the early 1920's that steps were really taken to arm racing with a security force of its own and to rid the courses of the race gangs which were bringing the sport into disrepute.

The First World War had dispersed many of the gangs of thieves and strong arm men who had frequented racecourses, but when racing resumed after the war, the old gangs re-formed, and some new ones were attracted to the game at a time when ex-servicemen with gratuities to spend and soul-shattering sights in the trenches of France to forget were flooding to the racecourses for relaxation.

Often gangs made monetary collections from bookmakers on the course on shallow pretexts, the bookie knowing full well that he would be beaten up if he did not contribute. There were some dreadful battles on racecourses between rival gangs with names like the Aldgate Gang, the Titanic Mob and the Birmingham Gang. In one notorious incident, the Birmingham Gang travelled south to Epsom to beat up the London Gang of East End Jews and Italians. They started a fight but discovered they had attacked the Sheffield Gang. They rushed back to London and another battle ensued as the London Gang got off the Epsom train at Victoria.

In 1921 racing journalist J.M.Dick of the Evening News, who had been writing about the dangers to the racegoing public, was attacked outside the Coronation Hotel, Newmarket, by a mob who badly bruised him and covered him with a revolting mixture of flour and yellow ochre. In 1925 the Jockey Club, whose Stewards had at first been indignant about the writings of those who had drawn attention to the sad state of affairs, took action, and after conferences with the Home Office and the Jockey Club, they set up a racecourse security organisation which gradually drove the gangs and many undesirables away from the courses.

Today the Jockey Club security organisation working from Portman Square, London, under Brigadier Henry Green, and in co-operation with police forces throughout the country, has ensured that rogues find it difficult to gain entrance to racecourses, and the English public can go racing without fear of molestation in a manner which is a remarkable contrast to the state of affairs which existed 50 years ago. There remains the problem of the card sharps who frequent trains to race meetings. We once watched a man lose just over £50 between Sandown Park and Waterloo Station in a game of cards which started innocently between two oldish and respectable men who said that they always had a little game of cards to decide who would pay for supper. Within a few minutes an Australian sitting in the compartment and obviously one of the gang had joined in, and then the mug was roped in. The warning given on race days at London station that "Passengers are warned not to play cards with strangers" is a sorry advertisement for racing, and it is time that the railways and racing took firm steps to rid the trains of these rogues.

America is a country that has grasped the nettle of racecourse security firmly. In 1946 the Thoroughbred Racing Associations, formed four years earlier to co-ordinate the interests of 22 founder tracks in promoting racing to the American public and establishing a set of standards, decided that it was essential for a security force to be established to meet the threat of invasion by racketeers plump with wartime black market money and now eyeing the vast sums being spent in leisure pursuits such as racing by demobilised servicemen.

The result was the Thoroughbred Racing Protective Bureau, with headquarters in New York and field offices in California, Ohio, Maryland, and New England, and officers and agents throughout the country looking for irregularities among stable staff or anyone connected with the day to day running of racing.

The stamping out of illegal bookmaking on the tracks or the transmission by radio of results and pari-mutuel prices from the tracks to off-course bookmakers features among the T.R.P.B.'s work, and they have built up a file at headquarters of more than 25,000 individuals who have been involved in any sort of trouble at race tracks, or have been suspected, together with in many instances their fingerprints. Continual exchange of information between the T.R.P.B. and local police forces have proved of great benefit both to the organisations for law and order within racing and in general.

The year 1945 in which no fewer than 26 cases of "ringing" were discovered—not to mention those that were not—prompted the T.R.P.B. to introduce the lip tattoo system. "Ringing" is the crime that was committed in the Running Rein and Francasal cases—the substitution of one horse for another. Today the lip of every horse racing at a T.R.A. track must bear a number that is implanted painlessly with dies and which is registered with the T.R.P.B. Checking the lip tattoo is standard procedure before a horse runs, and it is a dramatic tribute to the system that there has not been a single "ringer" at a T.R.A. track since the system was introduced.

The lip tattoo has also helped to cut out many of the cases of mistaken identity which occur from time to time on breeding farms, or when horses are in transit or at the sales paddocks. There have been a number of incidents in Europe in recent years when a yearling has been sold to an owner and the groom has collected the horse in the adjoining stall, or one similar in appearance. Usually the error has been discovered before long, and the respective horses returned to their rightful owners, but one wonders how many cases have gone undiscovered. Lip tattoos, imposed when a horse is a few months old, make identification a simple matter and it is surprising that more countries have not yet adopted the system.

The aspect of security on racecourses which occupies probably more time and money than any other is that of doping. There was a time on the English turf when the improvement of a horse's speed by the administration of dope was not forbidden by the rules, though it was frowned upon by the authorities.

At the turn of the century, English bookmakers were considerably shaken by the invasion of American horses, whose supporters used medication liberally and who collected many thousands of pounds as the result of the victories of horses whose staring eyes and lathered condition would today probably initiate a stewards enquiry before they were ever allowed to set foot on the track.

Today medication is permitted by few ruling bodies. Nearly everywhere the testing of the urine, sweat, saliva or in a very few cases, blood, of winners and placed horses is routine.

In countries where bookmakers provide the facility for opposing in the betting a horse which has been slowed down by drugs rather than speeded up in order to make it a winner, the racecourse analysts have to look for both accelerators and decelerators. There is far less of this slowing down of horses than newspaper headlines would suggest. Horses can run badly for a variety of reasons which they are not capable of conveying to their trainer or to the public–maybe the horse just did not get a wink of sleep last night, or he has a pain somewhere and does not feel like galloping flat out over a mile or so.

At Newmarket, English racing has a forensic laboratory second to none, devoted to the detection of drugs in horses and to the continual battle of keeping abreast of new drugs coming on the market. In recent years the Association of Racing Chemists of America, with affiliated members from other countries, and the British Equine Veterinary Association have enabled a wide exchange of information on the subject.

When one considers that about a thousand new drugs are registered every year, it is obvious that racing's laboratories around the world have plenty on their hands, but every time you read a newspaper story which suggests that a horse has been got at in order to slow it down, just pause a minute and think how you felt about going to work this morning. Horses cannot tell us when they do not feel like doing a job of work, and 9,999 times out of 10,000 that racing earns itself a lurid headline because of the ardour of some news agency reporter in chasing a speculative story after a short priced favourite has failed to live up to expectations, there is a good natural reason for what has happened.

Horses on the Move

Six miles above the Atlantic Ocean, a four engined Air France Boeing 707 pushes its way through clear skies towards America, high above the gale force winds making life difficult for the ships churning along the traditional routes below, high enough for some of the choicest bred horses in Europe to enjoy a trouble-free ride to new surroundings.

Emigration for the horse has been made easy. The jet plane does today what a ride in a horse box, followed by a railway journey, a traumatic experience with a dockside crane, perhaps six days or six months on a boat without any real exercise, then crane, train and road box did for many years on the less frequent occasions when one country decided to import the bloodstock of another.

International barriers have been broken down by modern methods of transport, but in the 18th century in England it was regional barriers that had to be overcome, and the fact that there was no easy means of transporting a horse from say Newmarket to York to run in a race, unless it walked on its own four feet.

This is exactly what the best horses did. From Newmarket to York is 188 miles, and it took ten days, including stops at inns. Probably all this road work contributed to the hardiness of the horses which feature in the records of meetings spread over a wide area during the 18th and 19th centuries. But it also severely limited the number of big races in which they could run.

In 1836, Lord Litchfield's horse Elis, fresh from a victory at Goodwood, shattered those who had taken a view that he could not be at Doncaster in time to run in the St. Leger by arriving in a horse drawn van, and went on to defeat 13 opponents.

At this time, men were working in County Durham towards the evolvement of a steam locomotive which would draw trains carrying people, baggage, and horses. Once steam traction became assured, the dandy cart which transported both carriage and horse, was soon developed, and it was not long before the first racehorses began to travel from meeting to meeting by train.

In England by the early part of the 20th century, the transport of racehorses had become an important and profitable part of rail traffic. Special trains composed of horse boxes were sent off to big race meetings from training centres, or smaller groups of horses were attached to passenger trains.

Already, Hungary's great mare Kincsem, winner of 54 races, had shown herself to be firmly in favour of rail travel, and probably hundreds of stable lads throughout the world had indicated their dislike for it, with the long waits in cold sidings, the clankings and bangings around strange junctions, the difficulty in finding drinking water for their horses, and beer and sandwiches for themselves. Travelling by rail is one thing when you can go by Pullman car and sleep in a warm bunk. Lying humped on a cold mattress in an ill–lit wagon with your horse looking down on you, his breath showing in the cold air, is another matter.

But this was the way the champions travelled. It is reported that Kincsem whinnied with pleasure whenever she saw a train, and the great Italian champion Ribot always travelled this way when he went abroad. Even when he visited England for the King George VI and Queen Elizabeth Stakes he made the bulk of the journey as far as Paris by train and then consented to go by plane. Kincsem–Ribot. Between them they were never beaten in 70 races and between them was the best part of a century, when rail travel was supreme for the horse.

In England, complete train loads of horse boxes were marshalled outside Newmarket by slow, plodding cart horses, towing the wagons into place before they set out for Haydock Park, Liverpool or Scotland. It was commonplace to see individual horse boxes, carrying hunters or racehorses, attached to express trains when they called at country stations. The railways had a phrase for it–tail traffic.

But in 1947 a revolution in racehorse transport started. Already increasing railway rates were driving horse traffic from this traditional means of transport to race meetings, and as wartime restrictions on petrol were relaxed, trainers turned increasingly to the road box. Then in October of that year, M. Marcel Boussac, president of the French Jockey Club, became the first man in Europe, and possibly the world, to fly horses to a race meeting. He entered three for the October meeting at Ascot, and flew them from France in his own Bristol Freighter plane, landing at Black-bushe Airport, some 15 miles west of Ascot. To set the seal on a successful operation, two of the three horses won their races. Air transport for racehorses was on its way.

Today some 4,000 horses a year are flown on the England-France-Ireland circuit alone, hundreds cross and re-cross America chasing the big prizes on the East and West Coasts, in Chicago and Florida; horses are shuttled between Australia and New Zealand; from Chile to Peru to Venezuela and Argentina.

What does the horse think about all this? Probably a good deal less than does the occasional owner who anxiously goes out to the airport to see his four-legged asset climb aboard a freighter. Nine times out of ten the horse immediately starts nibbling hay from a net thoughtfully provided by the somewhat rugged looking stewards in jodphurs and caps.

The fact is that air travel is a good deal easier on a horse than road travel. No sharp turns, or sudden brakings for old ladies at pedestrian crossings. The steady drone of the engines after take-off or the swish of the jets on one of the massive inter-continental planes is restful to most horses. Just occasionally something goes wrong in mid-air as it does on the road, but on the whole horses have proved themselves the calmest air travellers of the 20th century.

A horse who typifies the equine jet set is Sir Ivor, who raced in the colours of Mr Raymond R. Guest, former American Ambassador to Ireland. He probably spent more time in planes than any horse in the history of aviation. Foaled in America, he was flown to Ireland in a Boeing 707 to mature on that country's rich limestone land, won two of his first three races there as a two-year-old, and hopped into a plane to collect the valuable Grand Criterium at Longchamp.

Once back in Ireland, his trainer, Vincent O'Brien, decided that a winter in the mild climate of Italy would give Sir Ivor a good start to his three-year-old campaign, so off he went by plane and passed the months at Pisa, popular wintering place for many of Italy's best horses, with its pleasant temperature and almost invariably good going underfoot.

Came the Spring and Sir Ivor's air travel began in earnest. He was flown back to Ireland and from Ireland to England to win Ascot's Two Thousand Guineas Trial Stakes; back again to win the 2,000 Guineas at Newmarket. His third consecutive round-trip ticket ended in a victory in the Epsom Derby.

Then came one flight to England and two to France for him to finish third in the Eclipse Stakes, second in the Prix Henri Delamarre, and second to Vaguely Noble in Europe's supreme championship race, the Prix de l'Arc de Triomphe. Finally he climbed aboard a jet and went to America to win the Washington D.C. International. His last plane flight took him back to Ireland to stand at stud. And at the end of a year in which he covered thousands of miles by plane, Sir Ivor looked healthier and more contented than at any stage of his career–the complete traveller.

Even so, it is still somewhat surprising to see the way in which valuable thoroughbreds (Sir Ivor was insured for more than two million dollars) are treated like any other piece of freight on a trans-atlantic flight. Airlines developed the roll-on, roll-off technique for the quick loading and unloading of jet cargo planes, with freight strapped on to wooden pallets which are slid along roller-studded trollies onto a huge scissor lift, taken up to the level of the aircraft deck, and then rolled down the length of the aircraft to be firmly secured in place. Spare machinery parts, tanks full of live eels, crates of clothes, fresh oysters and caviar travel this way. So do horses.

Such is the weight of transatlantic air traffic for horses now that before the 1968 December Sales at Newmarket, bloodstock shipping agent Jim Peden, whose great-grandfather started the family company by hiring space for cavalry horses and racehorses on the paddle steamers which used to ply between Folkestone and Boulogne, chartered two Boeing 707 freighters to carry the purchases made by American owners and breeders at the world's biggest annual horse sale. At London Airport at 4 a.m. one morning we watched several million dollars' worth of horse being slid along the loading ramps and up into the hold of a huge plane for a journey to New York which would take them less time than if they were driven by road box from London to York or New York to Baltimore.

Who knows what barriers of international racing will be broken down as aircraft become faster and more capacious. In ten years' time the Argentinian horse which is flown to London Airport for a crack at the King George VI and Queen Elizabeth Stakes, or the American horse which is slipped into a jet freighter at J.F.Kennedy Airport and unloaded a few hours later ready to run in the Epsom Derby will be commonplace.

Epilogue

Are the Others Mad, and only England Sane?

It was never the intention that this book should have any political message. It started off as a gentle coast around the world of racing, and the hope is that the pictures and the material accumulated will have interested and entertained the reader.

But the further one delved into the racing industry of each country, the greater became the contrast between those countries which had come to grips with the problem of the amount of contribution that betting on horse racing should make to the sport and industry on which it relies for its existence and those countries in which no realistic contribution is made.

Take, for instance, South America. There countries such as Argentina and Brazil are continually losing their best horses to North America because the prize money in their own countries is not sufficient inducement to keep them at home. In Venezuela and Peru, the racing industry draws a reasonable income from betting, and the prize money is at a much higher level than in neighbouring countries. The public expect and get a better level of entertainment, the racecourse facilities are superb, and right down the scale to jockeys, work riders, blacksmiths and stable lads there is a better scale of remuneration.

In New Zealand they took the sensible step of abolishing bookmakers and establishing an off-course tote betting network as far back as 1922. Racegoers in New Zealand today go to the many and varied courses and enjoy their racing unaware of the fact that they are missing the pleasure of fighting their way through a mob of bookmakers and their runners to place a bet. They bet with the tote, the rate of deduction is 15 per cent, the racing industry thrives and progresses, and everyone has forgotten what it was like to have bookmakers occupying the best viewing places in front of the grandstand.

In Australia, the state governments have during the past few years gradually closed down off-course bookmakers and replaced them with tote betting offices. Prize money there is increasing every year, and the benefit is spread to all those involved in racing.

In Europe, the contrast between one country

which has taken the step of abolishing bookmakers and one that has not is enormous–France and England. In France, prize money is now running at about three times the level of that in England, and that country has become the centre of European racing. The best horses in every European country are now attracted to France to run for big money, depriving the tracks of their own countries of both star horses and top jockeys. Racegoers gravitate to the major tracks around Paris each Sunday, or in August to Deauville. More and more owners from England and Ireland are sending their horses to be trained in France, and that country is also proving a magnet for American owners, whose enjoyment of racing on England's varied tracks is not such a heavy argument for having their horses trained in Newmarket today now that a Chantilly-based horse has so much prize money to compete for on the Paris tracks and at Deauville.

None of this would matter too much if racing in England, as in every other country, was not part of the entertainment industry, competing with television, cinema, football, and an increasing number of participation recreations. Good horses draw good crowds, and this is truer in England than almost any country in the world. But we have now reached the situation in which it is necessary to go racing in France to see the best English horses in action.

And where the good horses go, the good jockeys go too. Even at English metropolitan meetings, the presence of Lester Piggott must sway a number of those people who like to see this great jockey in action as to whether or not they have a day at the races–at a Midlands or northern meeting he is a definite crowd drawer. But Lester's availability to English racing has been seriously reduced since French prize money started to climb and he took the sensible step of becoming a freelance. It is not unusual for him to ride on three days in one week in France, one of them being, of course, a Sunday.

Horses, jockeys, racegoers–all flocking out of England while we sit and do nothing about a proper return from betting to the industry around which the whole thing revolves. There are vociferous writers such as J.L.Manning of the Evening Standard and Mr Jack Logan of the Sporting Life who argue that racing is no more entitled to money from the betting that takes place on the sport than any other sport. This is incredible and dangerous rubbish. In every major racing country in the world, the sport that provides the facilities for betting gets a proper return from it. England cannot be right and everyone else wrong.

Bookmakers have done serious damage to English racing by their long battle against a reasonable amount from betting being ploughed back into racing. For years they made no contribution at all to racing. Then when the preliminaries to the Betting Levy Act, 1961, were taking place in the form of an investigation by the Peppiatt Committee, they formed an amenities fund which produced the paltry amount of £300,000 for racing.

This fund ceased when the Horserace Betting Levy Board came into existence in 1961. It was unfortunate that the Board did not immediately establish a form of levy based on turnover, but chose one which involved a basic charge plus varying amounts depending on a bookmaker's profit. It was also tragic that the Act said that in deciding on the levy, the Board should take into account the bookmakers' capacity to pay.

The Levy should, from the start, have been a levy on Britain's vast betting turnover and not on the profits of bookmakers. In the first five years of the levy, with betting turnover running at an estimated £1,000 million per annum, the Board received from bookmakers only £8.9m., while racing in France was receiving some £30m. annually.

Every year in the negotiations with the Levy Board, the Bookmakers' Committee sought to prove that the bookmakers' capacity to pay had been reached. One year they almost succeeded in convincing the members of the Board that the rate of levy should be reduced.

Then in October 1968, the Chancellor of the Exchequer stepped in and instituted a 2 1/2 per cent tax on betting turnover, which he increased to 5 per cent the following April. In one year, ending March 1969, the Government drew £38m. from betting on horse racing, while the Levy Board drew £2.8m. The bookmakers' arguments on their capacity to pay were knocked sideways. They paid. Most pass on their betting tax commitments to the public by varying rates of deduction from winning bets, and this is what they could always have done with their levy commitments.

It was not until Lord Wigg became chairman of the Levy Board that a levy based on turnover was instituted in 1968. But the money that the Government draws from betting on horse racing and that which the sport itself receives is now completely disproportionate. English racing faces an extremely serious financial crisis at a time when racing in other countries is forging ahead, and it is about time that all those who believe in a tote monopoly made a concerted effort to bring about the one thing that can help Britain to hold its place in the world of racing.

It is sometimes argued that the betting man in England is different to his counterpart in other countries, and that it would be wrong to deprive him of the opportunity of placing sixpenny each way trebles and other varied bets with back-street bookmakers. But given the large injection of capital which would be needed, the Tote in England has the ability and the know-how to produce a computerised betting system which would offer the man in the street a wider range of bets than in any other country in the world, unfettered by the scandalous limits which many small bookmakers impose on winning bets.

The tote in England has always suffered from lack of capital. It does an amazingly good job under conditions found nowhere else in the world– competition with bookmakers; betting all over the country right up to the start of the race, whether the backer is on the course or 800 miles away; provision of a tote service at meetings which last never more than five days, and often only one day; and wide fluctuations in demand for staff, with sometimes two meetings on a day and at other times 16, plus many point-to-points. It already offers a greater variety of bets than any other tote in the world.

It is vital that those who understand the situation and who realise the importance of a tote monopoly should concentrate their efforts to this end now. A Tote Monopoly Association should be formed, backed by all those in racing who are now going about saying that a tote monopoly is essential but who are doing nothing about it.

One of the first steps must be a process of educating members of Parliament and civil servants in the reasons for a monopoly–a sound racing industry instead of a milch cow; ease of tax collection and abolition of the betting tax evasion which is now being carried on by bookmakers on an ever-increasing scale; and straighter racing.

Owners, trainers, breeders, jockeys, racecourse owners should unite in this one cause and as soon as possible. The cry of vested interests will be heard. Of course it's a question of vested interests– vested in preventing the further decline of English racing as a spectacle and an entertainment. We cannot and must not remain the only major racing country which has not taken this step.

Or are all the others mad and England in her poverty, the sane one?

Contents Table

Introduction 5

The Racing Game 16

The Most Important Ingredient 22

The Strength of French Racing 41

Contrast of British Racing 46

Racing in Ireland–Part of Life 56

Germany–An Ability to Produce Good Horses 80

Italy's Contributions: Ribot and San Siro 83

Russian Racing, for Points 86

The Tradition of Hungarian Racing 89

The Scandinavian Circuit 90

The Jockeys' World 96

American Racing–a Multi-Million Dollar Business 113

The Betting Man 137

South America and 75,000 Thoroughbreds 145

South Africa, a Flourishing Industry, but Isolated 148

India 151

Japan–a Power to Come 153

Australia–Eating, Sleeping, Talking, Racing 168

New Zealand 173

The Jumping Game 188

Twelve of the Best 199

An Eye on the Criminal 207

Horses on the Move 212

Epilogue: Are the Others Mad, and only England Sane? 214

Acknowledgements

The author would like to acknowledge with grateful thanks the help given in compiling and editing material by Miss Dorothy Laird, Mr. Nevil Davidson, Mrs. Enid Webster and Miss Ann Usborne.

The photographs within the text are reproduced by kind permission of the following: W. Anderson, pages 88, 139; Dr. Bernstein, pages 151, 171; Bettman Archive, page 115; British Museum, pages 25, 50; W. Gordon Davis, page 52; Mary Evans, pages 44, 52, 189; Photo Giraudon, page 43; John Green-Smith, page 118; Robert Goodmann, page 170; London Express, page 192; Mansell Collection, pages 24, 55, 97; National Library of Australia, page 171; New Zealand Information Service, pages 174, 200; Press Association, page 98; Radio Times Hulton Picture Library, pages 24, 50, 55; W.W. Rouch, pages 200, 201, 202; Udo Schmidt, page 82; Athol Smith, Melbourne, page 17; Stud & Stable, pages 18, 25; Syndication International, page 151; Topix, pages 52, 192; Wairarapa Times-Age, page 174; Weidenfeld & Nicholson, page 200.

Content printed on:
Biber Blade woodfree, high-white, mat two side coated, 130 gm²
Cover printed on:
Biber Blade woodfree, high-white, glazed two side coated, 140 gm²

 Papierfabrik Biberist, Biberist, Switzerland

Photo-lithographs by Interrepro AG, Münchenstein Switzerland

Bound by Hch. Weber AG, Winterthur Switzerland

David Hedges has been in journalism and public relations for the past twenty years and a racing journalist for fifteen years. He started his career with the Express and Echo evening paper at Exeter, and while there graduated from "covering flower shows, funerals and fetes" to sports writing and doing the daily racing selections.
In 1951 he joined the racing staff of the Press Association in London as sub-editor and later as a racing reporter, covering meetings in many parts of the country. After five years with this news agency he joined the London Evening Standard, and in the latter part of his three years with the paper he became "Ajax" after understudying the veteran holder of that famous nom-de-plume, the late Jimmy Park.
David Hedges joined The Sporting Life in 1957 and contributed a regular racing news and gossip column from 1959 until April, 1964, when he was asked to become Director of the Racing Information Bureau, then being formed to handle publicity first for the Racecourse Association and then the Horserace Betting Levy Board. In November 1966 he became Press, Publicity and Advertising Officer to the Horserace Totalisator Board and Tote Investors Ltd., while continuing to contribute to racing journals on a freelance basis.
During his career David Hedges has travelled widely and covered racing in many countries. He has reported on nine of the last twelve runnings of the Washington D.C. International at Laurel, Maryland.
In 1970 he formed the International Racing Bureau with headquarters in London, handling publicity and communications for Jockey Clubs and race tracks in America, England, Australia, New Zealand, France, Germany, Italy, South Africa, Norway, Belgium and Spain.

Fred Mayer was born in Lucerne in 1933 and now lives in Zurich. He has contributed photographs to many magazines, including Look, National Geographic and Réalités. In 1968 he won an award from the Metropolitan Museum of Art in New York. He has traveled in many countries, including the United States, Russia, India, Japan, Australia, New Zealand, South America, Africa, and almost every part of Europe. His other books include Carlos and the Elephant, Chakkar: Polo Around the World, and the documentary Cuba (with Carlos Franqui).
"The first big race I photographed was the Epsom Derby. I had been entrusted with making a great on-the-spot account of this race. I was fascinated by the whole set-up and the goings-on alongside of and on the track, by the elegance of the spectators, by the carefree mood of those thousands of onlookers, by the queen and her suite, and also by the striptease, at sixpence, inside the house. It turned out to be a very decent account, and I resolved to photograph as many races as possible during my many trips. *I never had imagined that sports pictures should be so difficult to snap.* To capture that lightning speed, and that beauty of motion was no easy matter, even with the best of equipment. I tried almost all of Pentax's Asahi lenses, from 17 mm to 1.500 mm. I worked shutter speeds ranging from one eighth of a second to 1/1000th of a second in order to try and show the unique combination of speed and power in this type of sport. I made use of the Pentax reflex camera in order to obtain – with the use of those very long telephoto lenses – the most dramatic close-ups of horseman and mount. In bad weather I had Ektachrome high speed films developed up to 800 asa. I have been photographing for this book for well over four years now, and I have made a great deal of friends on these many trips."